VIEW
FROM THE
SEA

"There is a rapture on the lonely shore."
Byron

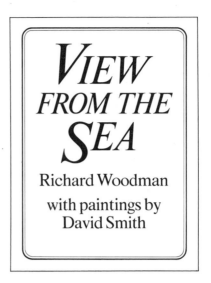

VIEW FROM THE SEA

Richard Woodman

with paintings by
David Smith

CENTURY PUBLISHING
LONDON

First published in Great Britain in 1985 by
Century Publishing Co. Ltd,
Portland House,
12-13 Greek Street, London W1V 5LE

Edited, designed and produced by
Shuckburgh Reynolds Ltd,
289 Westbourne Grove,
London W11 2QA

Woodman, Richard
    View from the sea.
    1. Coasts – England   2. England – Description
    and travel – 1971-
    I. Title   II. Smith, David
    914.2'04858   DA632

ISBN 0 7126 1024 3

Filmset by SX Composing Ltd, Rayleigh, Essex
Printed in Great Britain in 1985 by
Purnell & Sons (Book Production) Ltd., Paulton, Bristol

CONTENTS

South Stack, Anglesey.

For our wives

FOREWORD

Lowestoft.

Trinity House has served the seaman using English coastal waters for the last 470 years. The technology of ship navigation and the design of navigation aids may have changed dramatically in those years but the principle of setting seamen to provide for the needs of seamen remains just as relevant.

Trinity House is an interesting example of a very effective solution to the problem of providing a general service without putting a burden on the public purse and without burying it in the government bureaucracy. King Henry VIII hit upon the idea of a non-profit democratic company whose membership is limited to qualified professionals. With minor variations and a few critical periods, brought on by the usual foibles of human nature, the system has stood the test of time and continues to provide for the needs of seamen around our coasts.

In *View from the Sea* an artist and a seaman have combined to produce a book which looks at the coast as it is today and makes the point that, while safety of navigation is still just as important, the protection of this unique natural heritage is a responsibility of us all.

INTRODUCTION

South Bishop lighthouse.

David Smith and I came to create this book along very different paths. David had worked on subjects as diverse as industrial scenes and the glaciers and mountains of Antarctica before conceiving the idea of painting the coasts of his native land. He took as the focus for his new project the lighthouses that mark many of our most prominent headlands and from this inception our partnership began.

I met David when he joined the Trinity House Vessel *Winston Churchill* for one of her routine periods of sea-duty maintaining the seamarks off the coasts of Wales and the west of England. It proved an eventful fortnight. We covered most of our "parish", from the Irish Sea to the Chops of the Channel and were involved in a good cross-section of the many tasks that make up our particular business in great waters. We also had our fair share of a variety of weather from a calm to a fully-fledged Force 12 storm. My journal for Saturday, 7 January 1984 reads: "A full gale at noon from the Nor' West. The sea, containing much sediment, is a dirty colour, though the low winter sunlight throws shadows of the wave crests into the troughs ahead . . . I drew David's attention to it. He seems happy enough freezing on the after deck and drawing No 14 lightvessel in tow astern." It was clear to us both that, for quite different reasons, seamen and artists have at least one thing in common: their powers of observation are well developed because they are professionally necessary. Two days later the idea for this book was born.

My own interest is inseparable from my work of helping to maintain the navigation aids around our shores. Wind and weather still play an influential part here, and one cannot escape their effects or the necessity of observing them. The Trinity House service is relatively obscure. It fulfills its function without advertisement; yet thousands of ships and yachts make use of the numerous aids to navigation maintained by the Corporation. These, especially the lighthouses, naturally form the focal points in this survey of the coast. It is, admittedly, a highly subjective view, not designed as a navigational guide book, but as a source of enjoyment for specialist and general reader alike. The coasts of England and

Wales are impressively beautiful. As an island nation we are fortunate to possess them and although few are able to see them from our point of view, we trust that this book may in some way enable others to share our good fortune.

During his fortnight on board *Winston Churchill* David executed twelve large drawings, thirty portraits, forty sketches and watercolours. His energy and output were astounding, his enthusiasm apparently endless. To my astonishment he seemed to have drawn every corner of the ship without once getting in the way. Given the appalling weather that descended upon us during the second week at sea, the lively motion of the vessel and the physical difficulty of staying put, let alone drawing or painting, this was quite an achievement.

My journal for Wednesday, 11 January reads: "The wind gradually increased and backed until by noon it was WSW 9 to 10. At 1319 we drove in for Milford Haven, David sketching happily as huge seas pounded the red cliffs at St Ann's and the ship . . . rolling almost to the gunwhales with all deadlights down and the loose gear tumbling about below." We had been attempting to transfer the crews of lightvessels by boat and had to wait patiently in Milford Haven until the sea conditions improved sufficiently to enable us to launch one. Even here our problems were far from over: "Friday, 13 January 1984. Woken about 0245 by cable jumping on windlass. On bridge for rest of night. The wind was WSW 8 to 10, increasing in persistently long gusts of 50 to 55 knots towards dawn. Noted the date. 0615 Engines on stand by, in case. Furious sea, ship rolling, pitching and yawing. Coastal tanker close to shipping green seas. A dreadful night. Glass still falling at dawn. At 1000 wind veered to North by West 8 to 9." All this was in the "shelter" of an anchorage, but it was grist to David's mill and I distracted my anxiety by watching him draw the effect of a 50-knot wind on these so-called "sheltered" waters!

David's pictures were not only painted from my own ship. In addition to *Winston Churchill*, he sailed on *Mermaid* and *Stella*, sister ships operating in the North Sea and English Channel respectively. But the bulk of David's work was done at the lighthouses themselves. He has travelled by helicopter, car and on foot to some of the remote and lovely headlands around our shores, braving the caprice of the weather which was no kinder to him on land than it had been afloat. Fortunately his Antarctic experience stood him in good stead and he had long ago mastered the technique of pegging down his easel and coping with showers. For a seaman like myself, his pictures are full of the drama of the meeting of land and sea; what I suppose modern jargon would call "the littoral interface". The lighthouses have become part of the landscape itself, bathed in the tranquil light of sunset or under the shadow of an approaching depression.

This atmospheric approach is quintessential to my own view of the coastline. Lighthouses are interesting, historically and architecturally, but they were built to be seen, often in inaccessible spots, and time has imparted a unity with their surroundings. Their appearance at any given moment during daylight depends on the light itself and this is no less true of the surrounding land and sea. This effect is constantly changing, sometimes subtly, sometimes with bewildering rapidity. Its agents are wind and cloud and sunshine, and the ability to capture some of these moments is a rare skill. It is possible within the next half century that the advance of electronic navigational techniques will render many of the old visual aids redundant. Lighthouses will fall into disuse and some may join that growing number of sites labelled "industrial archaeology". Already many of the incredible skills developed in their building, particularly some of the masonry work, are all but extinct. They were built in an age when reliability, permanence and utility governed the production of such public works and the phrase "planned obsolescence" had yet to be thought of.

A view of the coast from seaward necessarily depends upon one's distance from the shore. A cliff seen close-to is an amazing collection of crevices, ledges, planes, fissures, lichens, seaweed, birds, nesting sites, rock plants and so on. From a distance of a few miles, under certain conditions of light, it may present a monotonous face which fades with distance until it dips below the horizon. But its presence may be felt many miles further seawards.

To a seaman the existence of land signals danger. It creates violent tidal streams and demands greater accuracy in navigation than the open ocean. This is an especial hazard when you are maintaining aids to navigation such as lighthouses. The very work of servicing these requires the attending vessel to be deliberately placed near danger, where no normally prudent shipmaster would go. But this adds spice to the work in which I have been involved for many years and which David was able to view at first hand.

There is, however, one drawback to this unique viewpoint and one which cannot escape comment. Already the coastal waters of Britain are showing irreversible signs of pollution. Thin films of oil are ever present and, although much of this eventually evaporates, there is more permanent rubbish such as plastic containers, fertilizer sacks, plastic bags, tyres, milk crates, archipelagoes of polystyrene packing, ropes, wood and many other more extraordinary items floating about, like contraceptives and traffic cones. Only a small percentage of this litter is the flotsam produced by shipping, most is from the conurbations of man, as any casual beachcomber can verify.

All this, then, forms the background of our book. We hope you will enjoy it and share with us the unique beauty of the coasts of England and Wales.

CHAPTER ONE

THE COASTWISE LIGHTS

The first land we saw, it was called the Dodman,
Then Rame Head, off Plymouth, Start, Portland and Wight,
We sailéd past Beachy, past Fairlight and Dungeness
And then bore away for the South Foreland light.

So runs the song *Spanish Ladies*, thought to be old when Nelson first went to sea and one of the loveliest of all sea-songs. After a commission in the waters of the Mediterranean a British man-o'-war runs up the English Channel. Making her landfall off Plymouth, she scuds up the coast with a favourable wind, her crew naming the most prominent headlands as she passes them, bound for the great anchorage of the Downs, tucked under the lee of the east coast of Kent.

Running up the Channel from a foreign voyage is no less exciting today than it was in the early eighteenth century when *Spanish Ladies* was first sung. There is a neurotic condition caused by the high excitement of a return after a long absence that is known among seamen as "The Channels". But today the mariner would be expected to traverse the French coast, following the mandatory routeing system which has made this busy sealane a marine motorway, with clearly defined lanes, central reservations and coastal slip-roads. When the British man-o'-war in the song ran eastwards, those lighthouses that she passed were privately owned, speculative ventures.

Today, although he is following the French coast, the modern sailor passes many signs of the work of Trinity House: the Casquets lighthouse, the Channel and East Channel lightvessels, which are off Alderney, and a string of Channel Separation buoys marking the central reservation between the main east and west flow of shipping. All these stations are maintained by the ancient Corporation of Trinity House, itself old when *Spanish Ladies* was first heard aboard a British ship. Some explanation of this curiously English state of affairs is called for.

Sir Winston Churchill once attended a wartime conference wearing a uniform unfamiliar to other Allied delegates. A French officer, who was curious to know the precise nature of the Prime Minister's dress, asked his British counterpart what it was. He was informed in impeccable French that it was the uniform of an Elder Brother of the Trinity House. The Frenchman was clearly impressed.

"*Mon Dieu!*" he is said to have exclaimed, "*Quelle influence!*" A similar tale is told about Gladstone who was elected an honorary Elder Brother towards the end of the last century. The news was carried by a Paris newspaper as something of a scoop. It was concluded that the old statesman's entry into a "religious order" marked his retirement from politics.

But it is not only foreigners who misunderstand this most curious of British institutions. During the seventeenth century Samuel Pepys, while serving in the high office of Master of the Corporation, complained of the ignorance of his own countrymen: "Why the name Trinity House is given to these societies of mariners hath been wondered at by many and indeed the name hath given occasion to sundry profane jests in common discourse and even in Parliament." In the intervening three centuries the situation has not changed very much. That particularly English love of traditional titles is apt to obscure the fact that today Trinity House maintains one of the world's foremost services to international shipping by marking the dangers that litter our coastal waters and extend many miles offshore in the comparative shallows of the continental shelf.

Apart from rocks, reefs, sandbanks, dangerous tidal conditions, the frequency of gale-force winds and blinding fogs, the waters around the British Isles cover an estimated quarter of a million wrecks. Although a fair proportion of these is due to enemy action in times of war, the vast majority simply attest to the ever-present dangers that confront men pursuing their business on the sea. Most major improvements in the safety of navigation only followed disasters, as we shall see. Even at the apogee of Victorian technical achievement and British maritime power, Kipling wrote with absolute accuracy:

> *We have fed our sea for a thousand years*
> *And she calls us, still unfed...*

Losses, in terms of British ships, cargoes and men, were indeed "The Price of Admiralty", and Kipling's poem of that name rightly points out that the main currency in which it was paid was the blood of seamen. The lives of both merchant and naval seamen were for many generations treated with prodigal indifference and it was often the loss of property, that is ships and cargoes, which prompted the influential merchant classes to call for improvements in coastal lighthouses, buoys and beacons.

The easiest seamarks to provide were simple wooden beacons, visible only in daylight. At night fires of wood, and later coal, were lit upon prominent headlands. The Romans built several light towers for this purpose. There are ruins of a Roman pharos at Dover and the present lighthouse at Corunna in northern Spain still incorporates much of the Roman masonry dating from the second century AD. But it was not until the Middle Ages, when the sea around Europe began to be used more for extensive commerce than piracy and military operations, that people began to look seriously at ways of providing seamarks for the mariner.

Early attempts at beacon-lights consisted of nothing more than wood fires lit in iron baskets and though these developed into coal grates mounted on stone towers, they remained crude indicators for many years. Their usefulness depended upon the maintenance of their fires at night and, since no one wanted the expense of doing this, they were usually provided by religious bodies as a philanthropic gesture. So early lighthouse keepers were often hermits or lay-brothers. One such light was maintained by an anchorite on the Ecrehou Reef in the Channel Islands as early as 1309, while the earliest reference to a lighthouse on the English mainland (excepting the Roman pharos at Dover) is to one at Winchelsea in 1261. This was probably kept by the local authorities, as Winchelsea then stood upon an inlet of the sea and was an important Cinque Port, trading in wines with the Angevin provinces in France. In common with the other Cinque ports, Winchelsea was allowed special privileges of trade in return for supplying the king with ships in time of war.

But such seemingly obvious steps were apparently not taken elsewhere. This was very likely due to the interest coast-dwellers had in encouraging wrecks as a means of ekeing out a subsistence economy during the winter months. English common law stated that the rights over wreck (that is ships, whales and sturgeon) belonged exclusively to the Crown (1324), although in places this right seems to have been passed to the local landowner if he was sufficiently influential. Vice-admirals of the coast were set up under the supervision of the lord-admiral to enforce this and until 1771 it was almost impossible for an owner to recover his property. In practice, of course, wrecks were usually looted long before either the admiralty officers or the owners were informed. A condition of the recovery of a wreck by its owner stipulated that persons should still be living aboard the wreck. How many half-drowned sailors were quietly murdered to evade this provision is unrecorded, but such ill-gotten gains were certainly much sought-after by the poor. Today customs officers act as "Receivers of Wreck" and life and property is, of course, fully protected by law.

Gradually there sprung up in the principal ports of the east coast a number of guilds, or "fraternities", of ship-owners and mariners who invoked the Holy Trinity for protection. They developed in influence with the growth of trade, and in wealth largely through their own endeavours and acumen. The first use of the name "Trinity House" is obscure and probably predates the earliest recorded House at Kingston-upon-Hull which was granted its royal charter by King Edward III in the fourteenth century. By the end of the Wars of the Roses in 1485, there were "Trinity Houses" in Leith, Newcastle-upon-Tyne, Kingston-upon-Hull and London. Their rise in influence marked the demise of the ancient Cinque Ports whose contribution of ships of war to the king ceased shortly afterwards.

The recent raising of the Tudor battleship *Mary Rose* from the ooze of Spithead has emphasized the significance of the Tudor navy and the part it played in the foreign policies of King Henry VIII. The maintenance of a standing naval force prompted better provisions for safe navigation and highlighted the need for some organization to be appointed to prevent foreigners, especially "Scots, Flemings and Frenchmen", from learning "the secrets of the King's streams". This persuaded Henry to grant special powers to the Trinity House of London. On 26 May 1514 a royal charter was granted, incorporating "our trewe and faithful subjects, shipmen and mariners of this our realm of England" to "begyn of new and erect or establish a Guild or Brotherhood of themselves or other persons as well men and women whatsoever they be . . ." Henry's provision for women is curious, but it is unlikely that he foresaw female emancipation and no woman was in fact ever appointed. The Corporation was to be governed by a Master, Warden and Assistants with its headquarters at Deptford. A revision of the charter carried out by James I renamed the Assistants "Elder Brethren", a name which has stuck ever since. Over the centuries the number of salaried Elder

The launch of the new Trinity House Vessel Patricia in 1982.

Brethren has altered and today there are eight. An important provision of the original charter empowered Trinity House to oversee the erection of seamarks, and it is this right which concerns us in tracing the development of aids to navigation around our coasts. The Jacobean charter also provided for additional guild members, known to this day as "Younger Brethren". About 250 remain, being masters in the Merchant Navy or officers in the Royal Navy. They have no executive function, but the Elder Brethren are elected from their number.

Despite the fact that King James I was sixth of that name to rule Scotland, his charter did not extend the powers of Trinity House north of the Tweed or the Solway. The Corporation is today responsible for the lighthouses of England,

Wales, the Channel Islands and Gibraltar. Scotland and the Isle of Man are the responsibility of the Commissioners for Northern Lighthouses, based in Edinburgh, whose foundation dates from a regulating Act of 1786. Coevally Ireland was similarly regulated, the Commissioners for Irish Lights running their service from Dublin and being responsible for the coasts of Eire and Ulster. These three authorities derive their income from a percentage of port duties levied on ships using British and Irish ports.

The first Master of Trinity House was Thomas Spert, who was also the sailing master, or chief navigator, of the *Mary Rose* and later of the pride of Henry VIII's fleet, the massive *Henri Grace à Dieu*, better known as the *Great Harry*. In its early days, as well as giving advice, Trinity House assisted the Navy Board in a variety of ways, ranging from the procurement of ships to the conservation of oak trees for shipbuilding. In 1588 ships and charts were provided for the attack on the Spanish Armada and despite its Royalist connections, Trinity House provided transports for Cromwell's Dunbar campaign of 1650. As late as the 1850s Trinity House was examining the masters and mates of the Royal Navy for their professional qualifications. Due to the lax regulations which governed the appointment of commissioned lieutenants, navigators for men-o'-war had been provided from the ranks of skilled professionals, usually from the merchant service. By the start of the nineteenth century the standard of navigation among junior naval officers had much improved and the non-commissioned masters and mates were dispensed with.

Revisions of the royal charter occurred regularly. Under King William III it was stipulated that no person could become an Elder Brother who had not been a seaman, waterman, fisherman, lighterman, bargeman or keelman. Although this effectively excluded women, it also prevented the common abuse of appointing place-seekers, jobbers and political opportunists. The Corporation became very wealthy, administering funds, often from bequests, in its own right, but not often spending them on the provision of seamarks. The Brethren did build and manage a few lighthouses – the one at Lowestoft, for instance, and the tower at St Agnes in the Isles of Scilly. But they were not alone. Private landowners also speculated in building lighthouses and collecting the light dues through agents in the various ports. This resulted in a vastly varying quality of reliability and service. While some owners became wealthy, others found it impossible to collect sufficient dues to maintain their lights, or to find men reliable enough to keep the fires burning brightly, without "excessive smoak".

Public insistence on the provision of lights at certain key points, most notably on the dangerous east coast where no landowner wanted to undertake the task, meant that Trinity House was often under pressure to assume the responsibility. Given that under the charters it was a right granted exclusively to them, this is not surprising. The Corporation, however, usually sought to evade the responsibility by acting as a consultative and licensing authority on the Crown's behalf. The system worked like this: when a landowner contemplated constructing a lighthouse for profit he petitioned the Crown for a patent and the petition was then forwarded to Trinity House. The basic requirement to satisfy the Brethren was that the light had to be demonstrably necessary (i.e. the petition had to have a number of signatories involved in shipping), and that there should be no possibility of its being confused with a neighbouring light. If the proposed lighthouse was felt to be of real benefit to seamen, then the Corporation would recommend the Crown to sanction the application and issue a patent. The patentee then paid Trinity House an annual rent as a form of licensing fee, whilst the Elder Brethren undertook a loose supervision. In almost all the agreements a lease was granted in which the lighthouse was to become the property of Trinity House in not less than ninety-nine years. Trinity House thus retained its prescriptive right; it eventually obtained a lighthouse, yet left the builder to profit during his own lifetime. An alternative method was for the Crown to grant the patent direct to Trinity House, who then negotiated with the petitioner as a lessee.

One of the reasons initially advanced by Trinity House to evade building lighthouses was lack of proper income. To solve this, during the reign of Elizabeth I, the monopoly of ballastage on the River Thames ceased to be a perquisite of the Lord High Admiral and was transferred to Trinity House. This meant that all ships taking in ballast after unloading in the London River, had to buy the shingle necessary to make them stable from Trinity House. Over the three hundred years of its existence, the Ballast Office of the Corporation earned a great deal of money, for the port of London prospered far beyond the dreams of Elizabeth and her advisers. Trinity House's income from ballast ended only in the nineteenth century with the introduction of iron and steel hulls with integral tanks for water-ballast. By this time, however, all English and Welsh lighthouses were under Trinity House control and all the light dues came to the Corporation instead of to private owners. Up until the abolition of private ownership in 1836 some owners had made enormous profits. Indeed the matter reached scandalous proportions at times and lengthy litigation took place in several instances over the amount of compensation offered to dispossessed owners. Writing *Nicholas Nickleby* in 1838 while some of these cases were going through the courts, Charles Dickens alluded to this. In pressing his attentions upon Nicholas's widowed and foolish mother, the lunatic tries to impress her with his imagined wealth: "I have estates, ma'am, jewels, lighthouses..."

Lighthouse ownership had been popular for many years, but it flourished particularly among the impoverished noblemen who returned with Charles II at the Restoration in 1660. This shrewd and penniless monarch encouraged the trend, seeing it as an inexpensive way of paying off his creditors, many of whom had ruined themselves in his service. More cynically, it also performed a public service for which Charles could take the credit. It was lucrative enough for Lord Grenville to write in his diary that he intended "to watch the King when he is in good temper to ask of him a lighthouse".

Above: A Cardinal buoy is made fast alongside a Trinity House Vessel. Below: Buoys stored on the foredeck for routine checking.

*Souter lighthouse stands on Lizard Point, slightly to the
north of Souter Point. The fluorescent red band is
designed to make the lighthouse stand out against the
surrounding buildings during daylight.*

The Act of Parliament of 1836 which abolished the remaining private lighthouses in England and Wales (none then existed in the other parts of the United Kingdom) also, of course, transferred the income from those lights to Trinity House in the form of light dues. Since that time Trinity House has assumed full responsibility for all the seamarks around the coasts of England and Wales, with the exception of a handful of major mercantile ports which maintain their own buoyed approaches. To carry out this duty Trinity House runs workshops, buoy yards, depots and a small fleet of lighthouse tenders, ships of around 2,000 tonnes gross, which service all those seamarks offshore. They are descended from a fleet of sailing vessels operated by the Corporation since about 1740. In 1835 Trinity House built its first steam tender, the paddle-wheeled *Vestal*. A hundred years later their first diesel-engined ship was commissioned, named *Strathearn* after Queen Victoria's son Arthur, Duke of Connaught and Strathearn, who was then the Master of Trinity House. His daughter, Lady Patricia Ramsay, has achieved the unusual distinction of having three successive ships named *Patricia* in her honour. The last was commissioned in 1982.

Today the business of the Corporation of Trinity House is more complex than ever. In addition to its national responsibilities, Trinity House has pioneered a new, internationally accepted, buoyage system. It is the result of a century of negotiations (gravely disrupted by two World Wars), which has helped to standardize the world's many national systems. Board members and officers of Trinity House give advice and practical help to under-developed countries, and for several years the Corporation mounted a protective operation in the Straits of Dover, designed to permit the national grids of the United Kingdom and France to share electric power, by policing the contractors' vessels and equipment while four trenches were dug and cables laid across the world's busiest sealane.

From its headquarters on Tower Hill in London, through the operational control centre at Harwich in Essex, via the sub-depots at Great Yarmouth, Cowes, Penzance, Swansea and Holyhead; through the helicopter crews, the crews of the tenders, the lighthouse keepers and men of the lightvessels, the hierarchy of Trinity House is thick with the strands of a long, proud tradition of service. Behind the apparent anachronisms a vital, modern service exists, underplayed as is typical of British institutions, almost self-effacing but extraordinarily resilient and amenable to change. In the age of high technology the pace of change is ever accelerating. To the basic function of exhibiting a light readily identifiable by a mariner, modern technology has added a variable selection of fog signals, radio beacons, radar responding beacons (racons) and so on. But during the greater part of the last two hundred years most of the alterations have been concerned with the visibility and reliability of the light itself. The simple open coal fires were improved first by burning them in grates, or "chauffers", of controllable design. Later these were sometimes enclosed in glazed lanterns. A coal light was in use at St Bees until 1822. The difficulties of supplying the first tower on the Eddystone with coal forced Winstanley to use candles in 1698.

Smeaton (1756) tried oil lamps but these proved too smoky and he, too, reverted to candles. Despite the achievement of building the tower on the wave-swept Eddystone, the light was not very successful.

Technology, however, was coming to the rescue. About 1782 a Swede named Ami Argand developed a smokeless oil lamp that burned with an increased brilliancy by being placed in a glass tube. When the argand lamp was fuelled by sperm oil its efficiency was still further improved and the flame from a small wick was judged to be at least seven times as bright as a single candle. At about this time the first parabolic reflectors were introduced which collected the diffusing rays and reflected them horizontally. They were known as catoptric reflectors.

It remained, however, to devise a method of distinguishing one light from another. This was particularly important with landfall lights, those first encountered by a mariner heading for the land after a long ocean passage. Up to the end of the eighteenth century, and for long afterwards in poorly equipped ships, navigation was very crude. We should not be misled by the unique achievements of Cook and the talented specialists he trained. It was nothing for a mariner to be sixty miles out in his latitude and to have only the vaguest notion of his longitude, so it is not surprising that the greatest hazard facing a seaman was making the comparatively narrow entrance to the English Channel, avoiding the Isles of Scilly and Cornwall to the north, and the rocks and reefs of Brittany and the Channel Islands to the south. The three main lighthouses for which he would be searching were St Agnes in the Isles of Scilly, the Lizard light on the south coast of Cornwall and the light on the Casquets near Alderney. Although they seem very distant from each other today, to the early navigators they were very close. The Elder Brethren were themselves practical seamen and they knew the worries and perils of such an approach. One of their own earliest lights had been at St Agnes (1690) and when construction of the Lizard and Casquets lighthouses began they solved the problem in the only way then open to them. They increased the number of fires, so that two towers were built at the Lizard and three at Casquets.

The difficulties the keepers then had to ensure each fire burned with equal intensity may best be imagined, but no other solution seemed to offer itself until another Swedish invention was introduced in about 1790. This was the brainchild of a man named Jonas Norberg, who devised a revolving optic, driven by clockwork, which would transmit a beam of light, or several beams of light, at a given rate right round the horizon. From the sea the light would only shine with intensity as the beam swept past the observer and by mounting combinations of argand burners and reflectors together a whole permutation of characters became available to lighthouse designers. A single flash, double flash or even a group of several flashes could be projected. There were also forms of hood made available so that a clockwork regulated shroud extinguished the light for short periods, making a range of occulting characters possible. Private owners were generally opposed to such costly innovations, but after 1836 they became universal. The height of a lighthouse lent itself admirably to the fitting of heavy weights descending in a tube to drive the mechanism, rather like a long-case clock. It was the keeper's duty to wind the weight up every half hour or so and mechanisms like this were in use as late as the 1970s. The motion of lightvessels delayed the fitting of revolving lights for some years, but eventually this too was achieved and further improvements in light intensity were made by introducing different oils, measured first in candlepower but today in the internationally recognized standard unit of the "candela". Vegetable oil followed sperm oil about 1845 and mineral oil came into use in 1873.

By the beginning of the twentieth century the properties of vaporized oil burnt in an incandescent burner had further increased the power of the light source and this was magnified by increasingly powerful lenses rather than reflectors. Early attempts at fitting lenses had been abandoned until the experiments of the Frenchman, Augustin Fresnel, proved successful. Basing these on theoretical deduction, he carried out practical trials which were largely ignored in his own lifetime, despite his being a member of both the Académie des Sciences and the Royal Society. But after his death in 1827 his ideas gained ground and were swiftly incorporated into the design of new lighthouses. The complex lenses known as "Fresnel Optics" were classified in several orders, depending on focal length, and were huge constructions, mounted in bronze frames weighing up to a ton and floating in mercury troughs. They were always kept in pristine condition and the whole apparatus was so beautifully made that they could be turned and free-wheeled by the application of a single finger. Like the incandescent burners, they remained in service until the 1970s and lighthouse keepers still lament their passing.

The rapid introduction of such improvements followed the 1836 Act empowering Trinity House to assume direct responsibility for all English and Welsh lights. With the characteristic energy of the Victorians in all engineering matters, which contrasts so much with the disinterest of their forefathers, it set about improving the quality of the whole service. These improvements were greatly helped by the timely introduction of steam power, not only for driving the ships that carried stores and building materials to lighthouse sites, but also in the construction itself. During the latter half of the nineteenth century lighthouse construction reached its apogee and is unlikely to be improved upon, if indeed it could now be equalled. The mariner's instruments were still basic, despite his practised skill with sextant and chronometer and the lighthouse came to signify reliability in a quite unprecedented way.

Progress also continued in other ways, and although it was 1977 before the last incandescent burner went out of service, electricity boosted the intensity of the lights still further. Curiously enough, electric light had been installed at Dungeness lighthouse over a century earlier, but it was discontinued due to the "incompetence" of the keepers. I have always felt this an unduly harsh judgement on these poor fellows who were obviously bemused by the first murmurings of our modern age. A few years later, in 1872, electricity was successfully supplied to the lighthouses at the North and South Forelands in Kent. Since then the improvements in the design and size of generating equipment has resulted in the installation of electric power at all lighthouses. Today there are no coal bags to hump, no grates to rake, no weights to wind up and, in many cases, no lenses to clean. One form of the modern gearless pedestal looks rather like a prosaic array of quartz-halogen car headlamps; but it is capable of sending out a beam of light in excess of one million candelas, visible up to thirty miles away on a dark night with a clear atmosphere.

Secondary unmanned and automatic lighthouses, beacons and buoys are usually powered by acetylene, the gas being retained in bottles under pressure and released through a regulator and a coder which produces the variety of flashing characters that mariners and yachtsmen take for granted. Electric power will, one day, doubtless replace it, but for the time being the simplicity and reliability of acetylene and its associated devices fulfill the demand of aids to navigation which, in the case of buoys, are subject to unimaginable violence in bad weather.

Possibly technology will make lighthouses themselves superfluous; already automation has made many keepers redundant. The advances made in electronics will doubtless one day make shipborne navigational aids so accurate and so cheap that the mariner will no longer need to stare at the horizon, searching for a glimpse of a landfall lighthouse winking at him in the dark. In his poem "The Coastwise Lights" Kipling makes the lighthouses speak for themselves in characteristically ringing tones:

> *Our brows are bound with spindrift and the weed is on our knees;*
> *Our lions are battered 'neath us by the swinging, smoking seas.*

Sadly, there is no longer that huge British merchant fleet which so impressed Kipling and called into being those magnificent Victorian light-towers. But although Kipling would have shed a post-imperial tear for the demise of the Merchant Navy, he might also have felt his heart quicken at the idea of transforming the sea into a source of energy and it is certain that he would have admired the technical achievements of the offshore industries.

It is perhaps not too pious to hope that mankind's common need to survive upon an exhausted planet may lead us to exploit the sea with a little more sense than we have plundered the land. The sea is less quiescent, less forgiving. Yet already there are serious signs of pollution about our shores which is irreversible. This, too, forms part of our view from the sea.

CHAPTER TWO

THE NORTH-EAST

Flamborough Head.

The east coast of England, reckoned from the Scottish border as far south as the Thames Estuary, falls into two distinct parts. North of the River Humber the coast is generally steep, with comparatively deep water close inshore. Although dangers exist, they are generally marked by lighthouses and few buoys are in evidence. South of the Humber the dangerous shallow water of the North Sea is ribbed with alternating sandbanks and channels running out from the great bulge of East Anglia, almost without a break, eastward to the Continent. Down this east coast ran Britain's earliest major shipping lane, roughly from the Forth and Tyne to the Thames, important from the late sixteenth century onwards and vital to London until the coming of the railways. As a consequence, the east coast became the nursery of British seamen, providing distinguished naval and merchant commanders, as well as candidates for that indispensible and appalling institution, the press-gang, which sent countless thousands of men to serve on British men-of-war during the dynastic wars of the eighteenth century and the great war with France which lasted almost continuously from 1792 until 1815.

Whilst the northern section of this coast could be rendered tolerably safe for navigation by the provision of lighthouses, the complex shoals and fairways of the southern part required a different form of seamark. Buoys have been used for the last three hundred years, and the modern lighted buoy which is also capable of bearing a radar responding beacon (a racon) is reliable. However, before the development of electronic navigational aids on board ship, seamen looked to the lighthouse authorities such as Trinity House to provide powerful visual seamarks offshore as well as on prominent headlands. It was thus that the lightvessel came into being. Variously called "floating-lights" or "alarm-vessels", the history of their development is interesting.

As early as 1679 a gentleman named Sir John Clayton suggested a moored vessel be anchored off the East Anglian coast with a fire-basket at her masthead. The idea found no favour with Trinity House and was dismissed. Sixty years later an adventurer named David Avery teamed up with an impecunious ship-owner named Robert Hamblin. Hamblin was a barber by trade, but was married to a lady who had inherited a single collier. Hamblin's management of the vessel was inept and his only profit seems to have been a knowledge of the dangers off the east coast. He conceived the idea (or possibly had heard of Clayton's original project) of fitting a vessel with a light. David Avery was a penniless but ambitious man. He was aware of the money to be made out of lighthouses but, being landless, unable to profit himself. Hearing of Hamblin's idea, he devised a

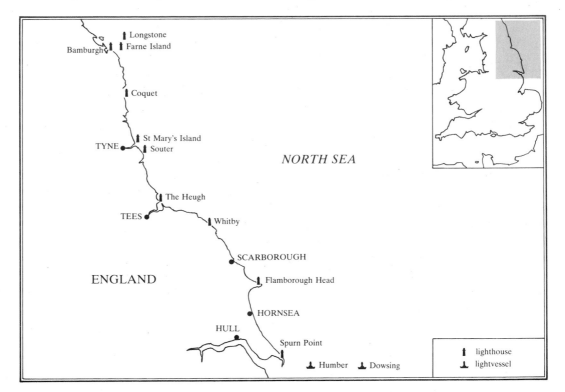

method of getting official sanction. Forming a partnership, they converted the small collier and fitted two fire-baskets at each end of a yard hoisted on a stumpy mast. Avery obtained a patent, circumventing Trinity House in the process, and moored his lightvessel at the Nore, where Thames and Medway converge. The Elder Brethren were furious and a long legal wrangle followed. The Admiralty refused to support Trinity House but the Brethren won the legal battle and orders for the removal of the lightvessel were issued.

Marine opinion was on Avery's side, as he had calculated. The removal of the lightship was greeted with dismay among the seafaring population who had come to rely upon it. Suitably penitent, the shrewd Avery now approached Trinity House with an application for a lease and a statement of "philanthropic" expenses he and Hamblin had incurred in establishing the light. Faced with a storm of public indignation, Trinity House allowed Avery the profitable management of the lightvessel until expiry of the lease in 1745 when they assumed ownership themselves. In 1736 Avery obtained permission for a second lightvessel to mark the Dudgeon shoal off Cromer. When it proved a success on such an exposed station, the establishment of further lightvessels was assured, reaching a total of fifty-four on station by the latter part of the last century. Since then the number has diminished, largely because of the increased efficiency of lighted buoys.

At the present time, lighthouses, lightvessels and buoys are still numerous on the east coast, but the first few miles south of the Scottish border, where we begin our tour of the coast of England and Wales, are comparatively free of offshore dangers until the Farne islands off Northumbria. The carboniferous cliffs that run south from Scotland, through which the River Tweed has incised its valley, give way to shales, limestone and thin coal seams. Beaches of sand alternate with rock outcrops along this low shore, while inland the ground rises to the rolling green of the Cheviot Hills. The southward end of Berwick Bay is composed of a sweep of sands, encompassing the low island of Lindisfarne, known now as Holy Island. The extensive sands that surround the island dry out at low water, allowing access via a causeway. The exposed sands are rich feeding grounds for numerous seabirds and waders, while the island itself, formed by a group of limestone plateaux linked by shingle, provides a habitat for grasses and wildflowers. Seals fish off the beaches and the island has been able to support human life for hundreds of years. The sanctification of Lindisfarne took place after AD 635 when King Oswald of Bernicia reunited the ancient kingdom of Northumbria and re-established the Christian religion by inviting St Columba's religious house on Iona to provide a man suitable to carry out the task. Columba sent Aidan, who established a monastery on Lindisfarne which survived until the ninth century when it was destroyed in a Danish raid. A priory was erected again in 1093 under the auspices of the Bishop of Durham and the ruins of its red sandstone church may still be seen.

The most imposing building on the island today is the castle built in 1550 as a refuge against marauding Scots. It was enlarged and embellished by Sir Edwin Lutyens in 1902 and more recently it was used by Roman Polanski in his film *Macbeth*. But Holy Island Castle is dwarfed by neighbouring Bamburgh Castle, situated three miles to the south, on the mainland, where an outcrop of the igneous dolerite, known as Whin Sill, forces its way through the local shales and sandstones. The seaward escarpment of the rock plunges steeply some two hundred feet to the white sands of the shoreline. Occupied by the Romans, it was King Oswald's grandfather, King Ida of Northumbria, who undertook the first embattlement at the beginning of the seventh century. Following Oswald's defeat by the Mercians at Maserfield (August 642), his body was hung on stakes above the gate. Northumbria took some time to recover from Oswald's defeat and

Bamburgh was sacked by the Danes. After the Norman Conquest, however, the castle was rebuilt and figures prominently in English history. In 1095 Robert Mowbray held it against King William Rufus. It was captured by the Scots, enlarged by Henry II and again improved by King John whose constable abused his position by robbing passing ships. A later constable was Harry Hotspur who led his army from Bamburgh to defeat the Scots at Homildon Hill, and it was to Bamburgh that the feeble Henry VI fled after the terrible defeat of the Lancastrians at Towton during the Wars of the Roses. In June 1464, after the battle of Hexham, it won the dubious distinction of becoming the first English castle to surrender to gunpowder.

By the late eighteenth century Bamburgh was largely a ruin and became a charity school administered by a Dr Sharp, a remarkable man who instituted a number of unusual measures to mitigate the dangers to seamen. Setting up a rudimentary lifeboat station in the village of Bamburgh, Sharp also directed that in fog and storms a bell should be rung and a gun fired from the ramparts as a guide to mariners. In addition, during gales two riders were employed to patrol the shore and summon help in case of shipwreck. Early nineteenth-century navigational handbooks, or rutters, gave seamen the comforting information that "dead bodies cast on shore are decently buried *gratis*", and that wrecked seamen would be respectably clothed and lodged for a week, while a premium was offered to any person reporting a wreck to the castle. Sharp's initiative was one of the first moves in recognizing the responsibilities of the community for safety at sea. His charity school existed until such works were taken over by the public authorities at the beginning of the present century. The castle was then bought by Lord Armstrong and restored to the condition it is in today.

Beneath the great ramparts of the castle huddles the village of Bamburgh with its church dedicated to St Aidan. Here, too, is a lavish Gothic memorial to Bamburgh's heroine, Grace Darling, born in 1815 in a cottage opposite the church. Five miles east of Bamburgh lie the Farne Islands where Grace's father was a lighthouse keeper. The little archipelago of a dozen islands is formed of scattered outcrops of the igneous Whin Sill. Until quite recently they were known as the Fern Islands, supposedly from the quantities of fern and bracken that grew upon them. The deep intersections or "sounds" between the islands are free of rocks but the tide rushes through them with dangerous speed. As is usual with offshore prominences, the islands have the effect of speeding up the coastal tidal stream and up to four knots may be experienced off the Longstone at the archipelago's eastern extreme. As the tide rushes past the obstructions, it causes large eddies or "indraughts" which can draw an unwary vessel towards danger. Even modern ships with radar are cautioned to avoid the area. At dawn on 7 September 1838 William Darling, the keeper on the Longstone lighthouse (then confusingly called the Outer Farne), observed a vessel driven ashore on the Harcar Rocks. The gale which had caused the ship's destruction was still blowing and the raging sea had already carried away the vessel's stern. She proved to be the auxiliary steam brigantine *Forfarshire* on her regular run up the east coast, bound from Hull to Dundee with sixty-three people on board. From the lighthouse Darling and his twenty-three-year-old daughter Grace could see the survivors huddling on the broken paddle-steamer's forecastle. The wreck had also been sighted from the mainland but the local fishermen had decided that it would be impossible for a small boat to get through the breaking seas around the wreck, or to risk a frail hull alongside the steamer amid the rocks. William Darling had reached the same conclusion. He had only a small, open boat at the lighthouse and it would have been a forlorn and foolhardy hope to attempt a rescue. The only likely result would be to leave his wife a widow and Grace and her brothers orphans. The girl, however, dared otherwise and volunteering to take the boat's second pair of oars, she persuaded her father to make the attempt.

One can only guess at the struggle they had to pull the little craft through the heavy seas and arrive alongside the wreck. Perhaps even more impressive was the return with five passengers, four men and a woman, cold, terrified and hungry. How were those five selected? There can have been little time for debate before William turned the boat and headed back towards the distant sanctuary of the lighthouse. Then, having set the survivors on shore, the Darlings made a second passage to the wreck and brought off a further four people. These nine were accommodated in the lighthouse for two days before the weather abated sufficiently for them to be landed. For their achievement the Royal Humane Society voted Grace and her father their gold medal; the government made them a grant and they became the beneficiaries of a public subscription. Sadly Grace died of tuberculosis at the age of twenty-seven.

The Farnes were so dangerous that they had been pin-pointed as a location for a lighthouse as early as the seventeenth century when Sir John Clayton, that inventively-minded gentleman with an eye for innovation as well as profit, began to petition Trinity House for the provision of such a seamark. The Elder Brethren equivocated and Clayton was left to construct a tower on the Inner Farne in 1670, but it was never lit because a typical wrangle over the finances broke out between Trinity House and the Blackett family to whom the islands were leased. It was not until 1778 that two private lights were built and exhibited by the islanders, one on the Inner Farne and one on Staple Island. Robert Darling, Grace's grandfather, became keeper of the Staple Island light in 1795. But this did not satisfy the navigational demands of the increasingly powerful mercantile lobby, who frequently complained about their efficiency and location. At this point Trinity House directed the Blacketts to fit argand lamps and reflectors which resulted in further arguments since, although Trinity House had taken over the lease of the lighthouses in 1786, they were apparently still relying upon the Blacketts to provide the hardware. Clearly this situation was impossible and in 1810 all parties renegotiated the terms of the lease and patent. Daniel Alexander, Trinity House's architect, organized the building of two new towers, one on the Inner Farne (now known as Farne Island lighthouse) and one on the Longstone. Trinity

House also took over management of the lights, compensating the Blacketts and retaining the islanders as keepers. The original tower on Staple Island was left with a fixed light; the apparatus at the Longstone revolved every half minute and was thus one of the world's earliest flashing lights. In 1822 an Act of Parliament enabled Trinity House to buy the site at a cost of £36,446 and in 1826 more work was undertaken to improve the Longstone and Farne lights. The white tower on the Farne Island is now an automatic station which throws a white light landward over the safer waters of the Inner Sound and a red light seawards over the reefs, rocks and islands, while the one on Staple Island has long since been discontinued. The Longstone was enlarged by Joseph Nelson and is a red and white circular tower built of rough stone with integral dwellings. It was built at a cost of £4,771, of which £1,441 was spent on the lantern alone which consisted of twelve-burner argand lamps, parabolic reflectors 21 inches in diameter and 9 inches deep. The whole thing was surrounded by a catadioptric lens. Further alterations were carried out subsequently, the most significant being the conversion to electric power in 1952. In addition to the white light that flashes from the lantern every twenty seconds, there is a fog signal and radio beacon which enables a vessel or yacht with a radio direction finder to obtain a bearing of the station by means of a radio signal. It thus operates over a much greater distance than a light and is unaffected by fog. Before taking our departure from this group of islands, it is worth noting that the Farnes support the largest breeding colony of Atlantic grey seals. The bulls can weigh up to 500lbs and both sexes can frequently be seen sunning themselves in a curious and characteristically curved posture, their heads and tails held up off the rocks – an apparently uncomfortable position which they hold for an extraordinarily long time.

The next coastal light, seventeen miles south of the Farne Islands, is on Coquet Island. The coast in between is low and undulating, but rises to high cliffs at Dunstanburgh and Cullernose where there are outcrops of Whin Sill. At Craster a water-cut haven was formerly used for the export of crushed rock for road-metalling. The layers of igneous rock form a series of shallow bays such as Embleton and Beadnell Bay, which all have their off-lying spurs of rock and reef. None of these dangers extends more than a mile offshore and the buoys marking them are of minor importance and unlit. From the sea the most imposing and conspicuous object is the ruin of Dunstanburgh Castle. Like Bamburgh, it has inspired several artists, including Turner, and was originally a fortified Saxon burgh. In the thirteenth century the site belonged to Simon de Montfort from whom it passed to the Earls of Lancaster and in 1313 the second Earl began building the castle which was gradually improved by his successors. During the ownership of John of Gaunt in about 1380, the great gate house was converted into a keep. In the next century, during the Wars of the Roses, Dunstanburgh was a Lancastrian stronghold and a refuge for the survivors of the bloody battle of Towton, but it fell to the Yorkists after the battle of Hexham in 1464. By the early 1500s, like so many others, it was declining in importance and was allowed to fall into ruin.

Offshore, three "seamounts" exist, named Dicky Shad, Craster Skeres and Newton Skere. "Skere" is an old dialect word for a reef of rock. They are not really dangerous, having some 70 metres of water over them even at the lowest tides, but, rising abruptly as they do, they are liable to produce heavy, breaking seas, known as "overfalls", when gale force winds oppose a strong tide, which are dangerous to small ships. They are comparatively rare on the east coast but we shall meet them frequently off the west coast of England and off the Welsh coast.

A few miles to the south, Alnmouth Bay opens out as the rivers Aln and Coquet empty into its waters. This is Percy country, the land of Harry Hotspur whose speech defect is unkindly reputed to have caused the rolling "r" of his Northumbrian descendants. The River Coquet forms a horseshoe loop round Warkworth Castle before debouching into the sea through the little port of Amble. Warkworth, which can be seen clearly from the sea, was Hotspur's birthplace and is a very complex fortress, despite the disparaging comment from Shakespeare's Henry IV who calls it "a worm-eaten hold of ragged stone". It was first built by Henry, Earl of Northumberland, son of David I of Scotland, and passed to the Percy family in 1332. When they rebelled against Henry IV, the king besieged and took the castle. But his son, Henry V, returned it to the Percys and it became a Yorkist castle during the Wars of the Roses. Henry VIII granted it to Lord Grey, his Lieutenant of the Borders, but in 1557 Queen Mary passed it back to Sir Thomas Percy who held it until his execution in 1569 after his rebellion against Elizabeth I. The castle then fell into decay.

Beyond the estuary of the Coquet River, spurs of rock run seawards to terminate in Hauxley Head and Coquet Island. Like the Farnes, Coquet was inhabited by hermits during the Middle Ages. In the twelfth century it was the refuge of a certain Henry the Hermit who is supposed to have adopted this mode of life as an alternative to the marriage his parents had arranged. He claimed that he received a divine revelation in a dream inducing him to take this action, though history does not relate whether the dream revealed the joys of the solitary life or the horrors of matrimony! The island is a low tract of grassland which almost doubles in size at low water when the rocky ledges from which the island rises lie exposed. It is a bird reserve and, particularly during the breeding season, puffins, kittiwakes, terns and many other species may be seen here in abundance.

The square lighthouse with its distinctive white and grey paintwork was built in 1841 to a design by the famous lighthouse engineer, James Walker, who was responsible for many of the lighthouses built after the Act of 1836. Constructed of sandstone with immensely thick walls, it cost £3,268. Like the Longstone, it is classed as a "rock station" by virtue of its isolation, the keepers being on duty for one month and ashore on leave for the next one, flying via helicopter from RAF Boulmer. The modernized optic exhibits a group of three flashes of white light over the clear water to seaward, with red sectors over the rock ledges adjacent to the island. When first built, the single keeper lived permanently on the island with his family and the first occupant of this post was Grace Darling's brother William. It is said that it was when she visited him there in the summer of 1842 that she caught a chill which turned into the consumption that killed her.

South of Hauxley, the coast is disfigured by open coal measures, though some efforts have been made to cover these at Druridge Bay. But from the sea the landscape becomes increasingly industrial as one moves south. It is no longer the geological formations that catch the eye, nor the habitations of our ancestors. From Newbiggin Ness to Redcar the land is fringed with chimneys and buildings, cranes and weird excrescences like cracking towers and flares. Smoke is not grey but every colour imaginable, including a brilliant orange miasma that drifts over the once lovely estuary of the Tees. Just south of Newbiggin the Wansbeck tumbles into Cambois Bay and three miles further south again the River Blyth emerges through its breakwaters. The shipbuilding town of Blyth is, like all the ports upon this section of the coast, severely affected by the recession. It was here that Trinity House built the steam tender *Ready*, the first non-belligerent ship to be constructed on the river after the Second World War. South of Blyth, the dunes are displaced by cliffs which culminate at Tynemouth with its conspicuous and ruined priory, built by Norman Benedictines and fortified by Richard II. Once marking the approaches to the Tyne from the north and dominating the holiday town of Whitley Bay, is St Mary's lighthouse on Bait Island. This is really no more than an off-lying reef connected to the mainland by a causeway accessible at low water. The tall white tower was built in 1898. During the excavation work for the foundations a number of skeletons in stone coffins were discovered, thought to have been monks from the adjacent priory at Tynemouth. The lighthouse was discontinued in 1984 and sold privately.

Tynemouth comprises two great stone breakwaters, each extending in an embracing curve and terminating in stone light beacons maintained by the Tyne Commissioners. Again in decline today, the river's history extends from the earliest recorded period. It was on its banks at Wallsend that the Romans started their wall and at Jarrow that the Venerable Bede wrote his *Ecclesiastical History of the English Nation*. Almost every type of ship to fly a British ensign has been built in one or other of the once world-famous but now sadly decayed yards upon its grim banks. The river exported the first "sea-cole" to reach London and her fleets of "Geordie Colliers", both brigs and barques, were well known. It was this burgeoning trade that prompted the establishment of so many of the east coast lighthouses and explains why lighthouses proliferated on the eastern side of the country and were so badly neglected on the west. But the most important contribution made by these little vessels was as a training school for generations of British seamen.

Above the entrance to the River Tyne stands a huge statue of Admiral Collingwood, Nelson's second-in-command at Trafalgar who inherited the Mediterranean fleet after the hero's death. In many ways Collingwood's own end was more tragic than Nelson's. A quiet, taciturn man, he had left home two years before Trafalgar and remained at sea until his death in 1810. He was refused leave by the Admiralty and died of a stomach rupture aggravated by the hours he was compelled to sit at his desk, administering his fleet and carrying out the delicate diplomacy then considered part and parcel of the duty of a commander-in-chief. On his rare visits home he had been in the habit of filling his pockets with acorns and scattering them on the ground so that oaks might grow to provide Britain with ships.

Of all the many hundreds of vessels to be built on the Tyne, one of the smallest remains one of the most significant. Although, as we have seen at Bamburgh, various places kept lifeboats, such operations were very much on a local basis. Seamen were plentiful and rarely accounted for much in the public consciousness. But in 1789 the sailing vessel *Adventure* failed to make the entrance to the Tyne in heavy weather, ran aground and was stranded within a few hundred yards of the shore. Thousands of spectators watched helplessly as the ship broke up and the crew were swept away in the breakers. Public apathy was, for a while, thrown aside and the people of Shields formed a committee, offering a prize for the design of a lifeboat capable of being launched and surviving in a rough sea. Two models appeared outstanding, one submitted by a teacher of singing, who was also a house-painter, called Henry Wouldhave, and the other by a boat-builder named Henry Greathead. Wouldhave's model was so designed that if it capsized it would immediately right itself. However, the committee were not satisfied that it would work (although the principle is now well established) and only gave Wouldhave half the prize. The first purpose-built lifeboat was then made by Greathead to a design concocted from several of those submitted. This boat had a very curved keel with raking stem and stern-posts and was rendered buoyant by seven hundred weights of cork. Named the *Original*, it entered service at North Shields and served for forty years, during which time it saved hundreds of lives.

South of the Tyne, the limestone cliffs are level, much populated by sea-birds. At Marsden there is a spectacular stack with an arch worn through it by the action of the sea. The area is dominated by the towns of South Shields and Sunderland which merge at Souter Point, half-way between the mouths of the Tyne and Wear, upon which Sunderland stands. Although named after Souter Point, the lighthouse here is in fact built upon Lizard Point, slightly to the north. After experimenting with electricity at Dungeness and the Forelands, Trinity House decided on completion of the building in 1871 to fit the new light at Souter with electric power. A scientist called Professor Holmes had "perfected a new alternating current machine", and two of these, each developing two kilowatts, were installed and proved highly successful, running until the station was updated in 1915. A second modernization took place in 1952 and has been followed by later modifications. Today Souter shows a red flashing light seawards every five seconds, with a narrow white sector over the inshore dangers off the entrance to the River Wear. To make the lighthouse more conspicuous by day (since it is set against a background of buildings), it is encircled by a fluorescent red band. Souter is also fitted with a racon, a radar responding device which, when triggered by an impulse from a ship's radar, transmits a tiny burst of energy. This is received by the ship on the same bearing as the point of origin and acts on the radar set as a received echo of exceptional length. On the ship's radar screen this will show up as a short but conspicuous dash, denominating the lighthouse which would otherwise be lost among the many echoes thrown back from the land, surrounding buildings and so on. It is, of course, also of great use in fog.

South of Sunderland, there is a rocky patch off Seaham after which a ship may coast safely down to Tees Bay with the magnesian limestone outcrop of The Heugh opening out to starboard. Forming a natural defence against the worst of northerly gales, The Heugh encloses the port of Hartlepool. Pronounced ''Yuff'', The Heugh is the site of a lighthouse and dominates the depressed port. This stretch of low coast is disfigured by the ruins of coal-mining. Yet it has an interesting history. It was from here that Crusaders sailed for the Holy Land and here that Aidan sent men to found a monastery. Hartlepool also possesses St Hilda's church, a magnificent example of Early English architecture. Badly hit in the depression of the 1930s, the town is again suffering from unemployment. One scheme to alleviate this is the restoration of HMS *Warrior*, Britain's first ironclad warship. This auxiliary steam frigate was for many years an oiling-hulk at Pembroke Dock in Milford Haven.

The vast sweep of Tees Bay that is enclosed by The Heugh to the north is bounded to the south by a long reef known as the Saltscar, off Redcar. This dangerous rock formation is marked by a buoy of the largest class. The final miles of the River Tees are one industrial complex of exhausted shipyards, thriving chemical works, refineries, steel works and all the heavy industrial processes of our age. In its lower reaches the river runs filthily between its banks and a foul miasma hangs over it. No self-respecting seal can be seen on Seal Sands and for my money, the Tees is the most depressing river in the land, a poignant contrast to its upper waters which are renowned for their beauty. Its lower banks do not show just the tired desuetude of outworn industry, like the Mersey, nor yet a civic effort to convert the eyesores of yesterday's decay into tomorrow's picnic spots as may be found on the Tyne. The last miles of the Tees are evidence only of the voracious appetites of our world and of the probable shape of a forbidding future.

To the south, the flood-plain of the Tees is terminated by the escarpment of the Cleveland Hills. As abruptly as it started, the industrial coast vanishes, and the great cliffs of Yorkshire rise up to border the North Sea. East of Redcar are the red-grey crags of Boulby Cliff, once the highest cliff in England but reduced by the hand of man through two hundred and twenty years of alum mining. Formerly shipped out through the now unnavigable reefs of Hummersea Scar, alum was once used for dyeing, the sizing of paper and the tanning of leather. Until the execution of King Charles I, alum production was a Crown monopoly. Nevertheless, the north coast of Yorkshire is a magnificent stretch of dark cliff, rolling inland as open moor which changes colour with the advance of the seasons and the play of light and clouds. From the Saltscar to Flamborough Head, the coast is comparatively steep-to. Small re-entrant, glacially-formed valleys, now watered by streams, break up the cliff-line. Runswick Bay has suffered from erosion and a whole village here was lost to the sea in 1682. A few miles south-east, the River Esk forms the little port of Whitby which produced two of Britain's greatest seamen.

James Cook was born in Marton, near Middlesbrough, in 1722. As a youth he was apprenticed to a Whitby ship-owner named Walker and learned his trade in Geordie colliers. He rose to be mate and then decided to volunteer for the Royal Navy where he was rated able-seaman. His abilities quickly attracted notice and he was patronized by Sir Hugh Palliser and Sir Joseph Banks, the mastermind behind British exploration of the South Pacific Ocean. Eventually commissioned as lieutenant, Cook was put in command of the *Endeavour*, a small, converted Whitby-built collier, and made the first of his remarkable voyages. Despite his achievements, the Admiralty were reluctant to promote Cook to the rank of captain. He was a "tarpaulin officer", not possessed of the social graces of a gentleman. The fact that he was a brilliant navigator, expert surveyor and no mean astronomer cut precious little ice. Even his patron, Palliser, who was well acquainted with his talents, dismissed a complaint by Cook on the grounds that his experience and knowledge were insufficient! Cook had criticized the quality of much of the equipment supplied him by the Royal Dockyards, comparing it with the superior standard of gear in the merchant service. Palliser was Comptroller of the Navy and responsible for such matters, an office notorious for the corruption of its officials and the jobbing of their minions. But the Admiralty did promote Cook for what turned out to be his last voyage. His death on the beach at Hawaii was a terrible tragedy, depriving Britain of a remarkable man. The musket which he carried at the time of his death is now in the possession of the Trinity House at Hull.

Whitby's second famous son is less well-known, yet followed a parallel career as seaman and scientist. William Scoresby Junior was fortunate in having a more influential father to whom he owed quick advancement. Both the Scoresbys were whaling men, living during the brief heyday of Arctic whaling from the Yorkshire ports of Whitby and Hull which lasted for a mere eighty years, starting in the 1750s. Leaving home in the spring, the ships would hunt seals and walrus while they waited for the ice to break up in the thaw, so that they could pursue the Greenland Right Whale, *Balaena Mysticetus*, for its baleen and blubber. The baleen, the krill-straining fibrous plates that filled the whale's mouth, were used in the manufacture of a variety of artefacts from corset "bones" to umbrella-frames, while the blubber was rendered down to produce lamp oil. Compared with the sperm whale fishery of the South Pacific made famous by Herman Melville's *Moby Dick*, the Arctic fishery has been largely forgotten. The Right Whale was far less ferocious than the sperm, although there are many records of boats being overset. Nor was it necessary for the blubber to be boiled down at sea. It was forced into casks and brought home to be rendered down in coppers at Whitby and Hull. A voyage to the South Pacific might last three or four years, whereas one to the Arctic was usually over in six months. But the conditions, even in the Arctic summer, were often appalling and it was not uncommon for whale-ships to be set fast and forced to winter north of the Arctic circle.

William Scoresby rapidly rose under his father's command and then became master of his own ship. He was so successful as a whaler that his ship accounted for one-fifth of the total whales taken between 1750 and 1830. Yet he retired from the sea in his thirties to become a parish priest in south Devon. Of a scientific turn of mind, obsessively enquiring and an acute observer, he was one of those God-fearing sailors who are the antithesis of their more colourful colleagues who provide the public with its traditional image of Jolly Jack. He refused to lower his boats after whales on a Sunday, demonstrating that he obtained greater catches during the week by observing the Lord's Day! His *History of the Arctic Regions* still makes compelling reading and in his account of a whaling voyage in 1822 when he commanded the *Baffin*, he describes his discoveries on the coast of Greenland that now bear his name. The achievements of Scoresby and his fellows enabled the streets of Whitby to be illuminated by whale-oil gas as early as 1825.

Overlooking Whitby and dominating the skyline, stands the ruin of Whitby Abbey. Danes, Vikings, Henry VIII's officers and the Imperial German Navy all had a hand in reducing it to its present state. The steps that lead up to it were used by Bram Stoker in his classic horror story *Dracula*. A mile further along the cliff stands Whitby High lighthouse, built in 1858 to another design by James Walker. Many of these early cliff-top lights were later replaced because they were so often shrouded in the mist caused by orographic cloud. Whitby has very largely avoided this by being on a predominantly lee coast. The original intention was for the tower to be one of a pair forming a transit over the off-lying danger of Whitby Rock. Nowadays the rock is marked by a bell-buoy and a red sector from the remaining lighthouse. The original back light, the higher, was demolished in 1890 when the low light was converted. Today, the lighthouse's main light is of an isophase character – that is, one having equal periods of light and darkness.

Robin Hood's Bay to the south of Whitby forms a picturesque indentation in the coast and is supposed to have been the scene of a battle in which the famous outlaw assisted locals to repel a Viking raid, a claim which confuses the historical evidence for his existence but is a pleasantly romantic story. From Ravenscar to the southwards the coast is high, with red cliffs which suffer badly from erosion. The more resistant sandstone at Scarborough has isolated the mighty rock there. The prominence was first used as a Roman beacon point and later the Vikings must have fortified it, for it takes its name from the Viking for "the strong place of Skarthi". Scarborough's present castle dates from 1136 and its main keep was built by Henry II. During the Civil War of the seventeenth century, castle and town held out for the King. Besieged by Parliamentary forces under Sir John

Above: The evening light over the North Sea can give it an unexpected sparkle. Below: Shipping in the North Sea.

Above: There has been a port at the mouth of the River Wear for over a thousand years. Sunderland remains one of the largest towns on this stretch of coast but its once prosperous ship-building industry has declined. Below: Spurn Head lighthouse stands on the lonely spit of sand and shingle that curves into the Humber Estuary. A wild and windswept spot, it is now a nature reserve run by the Yorkshire Naturalists' Trust.

Meldrum, it eventually surrendered in July 1645 when the garrison marched out in good order. Meldrum was mortally wounded in one of the assaults but his name will occur again in our story.

The land continues southwards as high and rugged Jurassic cliffs, terminating in the long, low finger of Lower Calcareous Grit that extends seawards in the rock formation known as Filey Brigg. The Brigg, which marks the north end of Filey Bay, has been marked by a first-class buoy since 1850 for numerous coasting vessels used to be lost on the rocks due to the sweep of the flood tide over it and into the bay. Filey Bay is cut in boulder clay and from its southern end the coast again rises in dramatic cliffs, but these are more severely eroded, being of chalk, protruding out into the North Sea in the huge salient of Flamborough Head.

Flamborough Head marks a great geological change in both the coast and the seabed. A line drawn across the North Sea between Flamborough and the Horns Reef, off Denmark, delineates approximately the rise in the seabed. South of this line the sea shallows to about half its former depth, rising firstly to the Dogger Bank and then to the long, lenticular shoals that lie parallel to the eastward bulge of Norfolk, gradually funnelling into the Strait of Dover. This change affects several things, most notably the tides and the character of the sea itself, producing waves with a shorter period between crests and, in heavy weather, a more vicious nature. The profile of these waves (known to seamen as "seas" rather than "waves") is altered appreciably when the tide opposes the wind, making them steeper and sharper, with a greater tendency to break. It is the breaking of seas that endangers ships. The water in the crest of a wave is highly aerated and has no buoyancy, therefore the hull of a ship does not rise to it and if the seas are big enough and break on board they can do a great deal of damage. The effect of a headland protruding seawards is also important. Where the tide flows along a coast at a steady rate and is then forced round a headland, its velocity increases substantially, often causing the overfalls described earlier at the Farne Islands. Many bays enclosed by headlands have dangerous overfalls off those headlands but, because of the movement of tidal flow from headland to headland, there is usually very little direction felt in the tidal movement within the bight of the bay itself. This effect of an accelerated tidal flow causes overfalls off Flamborough, particularly in the winter when a northerly gale often opposes an ebb tide flowing from the south.

The impressive chalk cliffs of Flamborough are the home of many nesting seabirds during the spring. Over thirty breeding species have been recorded, including puffins, razorbills, guillemots and kittiwakes. There is also the only colony of gannets in England. These magnificent pelagic birds are among the largest British marine predators and plummet to the sea from over a hundred feet in pursuit of mackerel. But even they can be harried by the voracious skuas. The dark shape of the great skua with its pale wing flash is frequently accompanied hereabouts by its smaller, long-tailed cousin, the Arctic skua. The great skua will make no scruple to attack a gannet until it has vomited up its crop for the benefit of the bully. (When a seabird is attacked, it will often vomit up its last meal, so lightening itself for a quick escape.)

The lighthouse at Flamborough has a somewhat chequered history. A tower was erected upon the headland by the ubiquitous Sir John Clayton in 1669, but no light was shown from the point for over one hundred and thirty years, despite the fact that one derivation of the name is said to be "strong place of the flame". In the Domesday Book the location is spelt "Flaneberg", which may be a corruption of the Saxon "flaen", meaning a dart. Whatever the origin, the headland has always seemed to me to be shaped like the nose of a head looking east, with the forehead starting at Redcar and a bearded chin terminating at Spurn.

Early seacharts called Clayton's tower a "lighthouse", which was the kind of misleading geography that led a certain Thomas Hood to say of those who drew them: "As for myself, I will not give a fart for all their cosmography, for I can tell you more about it than all the cosmographers in the world." This sounds like the authentic voice of experience when up against the academics! After about 1680 charts bore such legends as, "a lighthouse but no fire kept in it", or the more optimistic, "a high lighthouse but doth not burn as yet". Clayton gave up the enterprise in 1678. His tower still remains but he never had the sanction to show a light.

The present lighthouse was designed by Samuel Wyatt, architect of the first Trinity House to stand on Tower Hill, and was built by John Matson of Bridlington in 1806 at a cost of £8,000. At the suggestion of a certain Benjamin Milne, the Customs Agent at Bridlington, a revolutionary new lighting apparatus was installed. This was designed by one George Robinson and comprised a rotating mounting to which were fitted twenty-one parabolic reflectors, in three banks of seven. One of these banks was covered by red glass which gave a light character of three flashes, two of white, followed by one of red. Despite the fact that the red was only 60 per cent the brilliance of white and could not be seen much more than twelve miles away, the innovation was quickly adopted elsewhere. It is remarkable that the white light so obtained was recorded at just under 14,000 candlepower. Today's light is rated at three and a half million candelas.

Flamborough Head is an outcrop of pre-glacial coastline and to the southward lie the newer sedimentary rocks of south-east England. The North Sea once lapped the edges of the Yorkshire and Lincolnshire Wolds and the wide coastal plains to the eastward of these rolling hills which extend as far south as the Wash may be regarded as a gift from the Ice Age. But now the sea is bent on reclaiming its own. The low cliffs south of Bridlington are soft and offer no resistance to erosion. In fact they form the most eroded coast in Britain and the coastal waters are no longer steep-to. Shallow water extends seawards as far south as Cromer, on East Anglia's bulge. In the days when Cook served in Geordie colliers the haul from Flamborough to Cromer through these shallows, subject as it was (and still is) to gales and rough seas, caused the loss of many ships.

There is a phenomenon which is continuous along the coast from this point southwards to the Thames Estuary known as spoil drift. Despite the fact that the tides ebb and flow in opposing directions, eroded material, or "spoil" is moved southwards, often, as we shall see, with dramatic results. The first encounter with this is at Spurn Head. The spur of sand is very narrow and frequently breached by the sea, reforming itself a few yards further westwards. It is an isolated spot, the keeper at its automatic lighthouse (officially only an "attendant") being a member of the lifeboat crew. The Spurn Head lifeboat is unique in having the only fully paid crew employed by the Royal National Lifeboat Institution because of its remote location.

The mighty River Humber is said to contain two million tons of sediment at any given moment suspended in its waters. It has cut a deep channel through the sands that accumulate south of Spurn Head and is marked by the Trinity House lightvessel on the Humber station. The constant shifting of the sands and the convenience of the estuary, not merely as a means of access to Hull, Grimsby, Immingham, Goole and Killingholme, but as a refuge in heavy weather, prompted the building of the lighthouse on Spurn Head. The headland has been inhabited from about 670 when a small monastery was founded, but the long history of the light begins in 1427 when Richard Reedbarrowe, a hermit of Ravenspurne "havying compassion and pitee of the Christian people that oft times are there perished … hath begun in way of charity, in salvation of Christian people, Gods and Merchandise coming into Humber, to make a Tower to be upon daylight a ready Beacon, wherein shall be light giving by night, to all the Vessels that come into the said River of Humber." In about 1608 the sea breached the spit but by 1672 a new tower burning a coal fire was shown from the point and royal approval had been granted to levy a toll on passing ships for its upkeep. The London Trinity House had opposed the establishment of this light but the Trinity Houses of Hull and Newcastle had succumbed to bribes of £80 and £40 which "caused the London Trinity House to rue its opposition". The reason for this opposition is not clear but was probably because the proposal came from an outsider. It seems that the site was chosen by three gentlemen from Newcastle and the dues were one half-penny per ton. Coal for the light was expensive and specially chosen, being delivered by a Newcastle collier on the beach and carted over the shingle by oxen who were frequently lamed by the task. During the great storm of 1703 the coal burned so fiercely that the iron grate bars melted.

A shifting of the sands in 1766 led to a demand for improved lights but the patentee, one John Angell, shut himself in his house and refused to discuss the matter. However, his partner, Leonard Thompson, agreed to meet the Elder Brethren from London whose attitude had changed dramatically. An Act of Parliament was passed sanctioning the construction of two "swapes", coal baskets on levers which lowered the fires for tending, then swung them aloft again. These swapes were designed by John Smeaton whom we shall meet again at the Eddystone lighthouse. The two swapes were set up so that their transit led a ship through the fairway. The larger one was built on rollers which ran on a paved track and so could be moved to alter the alignment of the lights to conform with the shifting channels. But this ingenious arrangement was only temporary and on 5 September 1776 brick towers 90 and 50 feet high were inaugurated. Alignment of the two towers led ships down river towards Spurn Point. Illumination was provided by enclosed lanterns with properly designed grates whose intake of air kept the coal at a white and luminous heat. Smeaton wrote of them that they were "an amazing light to the entire satisfaction of all beholders ... vessels going round the Point in a dark night have the shades of their masts and ropes cast upon their decks." These coal grates were not replaced until 1819 when oil lamps were substituted. Upon the passing of the 1836 Act the Corporation found itself in dispute over the amount of compensation payable to Spurn's owners. The matter went to arbitration and was settled five years later when no less than £309,531 was paid out! Spurn Head is now reduced to a single tower, fully automated and showing sector lights over the various dangers in the Humber's mouth.

On the entire east coast of England only the Humber and Harwich form true refuges for vessels to anchor in during bad weather. The anchorage in the Spurn's lee known as Hawke Road is frequently crowded when a winter northerly sweeps at gale force down the North Sea and many masters seek shelter there rather than expose their ships and risk damage to their cargoes. It is also off the Humber that the gas fields of the southern North Sea begin. Offshore lie the Rough and West Sole Fields, both producing gas for domestic and industrial consumption, sending it ashore via pipelines that reach the coast a few miles from Spurn Head at Easington.

Steaming south-east the coast recedes into the distance. Unless making for the small ports of the Wash, a ship must make a greater offing to keep clear of the shallow water off Lincolnshire. Up on the bridge the officer-of-the-watch no longer looks for lighthouses. He watches now for lightvessels and buoys marking the unseen dangers of the Dowsing, Dudgeon and Haisbro Sands.

CHAPTER THREE
SANDBANKS AND SHOAL WATER

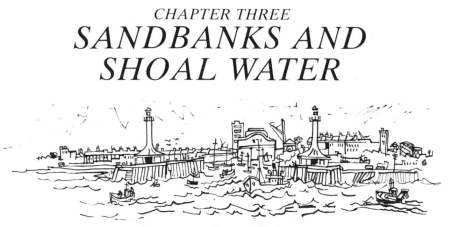

The entrance to Lowestoft Harbour.

The south bank of the River Humber, opposite Spurn Point, lacks any salient feature. The industrial and dockland area of Killingholme, Immingham and Grimsby gives way to the flat sands of Cleethorpes, curving round to the south at Donna Nook. From Donna Nook to the Wash, the flat coastal plain of Lincolnshire is an alluvial deposit inherited from the last Ice Age. As in Yorkshire, the original coastline is marked inland by a line of hills, now called the Lincolnshire Wolds. Shallow water extends well offshore along the whole of the Lincolnshire coast, providing fishing grounds and bombing ranges. The eastern extent of this shoaling is marked by the Inner Dowsing Tower, a former prospecting rig converted to a lighthouse complete with helipad, which rises on stilt-like legs some ten miles east of the town of Mablethorpe. In common with all "rock" lighthouses (a name deriving from their isolation and not necessarily from their actual foundations), the Inner Dowsing has a crew of three men on duty at any one time, who serve one month offshore and one month at home. Some of these stations have been fully automated, but those that are still manned continue a long tradition of care for the brilliance of the optics, the routine checking of the generators, the air compressors for the fog-signal and any other equipment. Keepers also maintain weather recordings, many of which are regularly forwarded to the Meteorological Office. In addition there are the domestic chores of keeping the tower clean and informing the Operations Control Centre of its fuel level.

At Gibraltar Point, just south of Mablethorpe, the coast swings abruptly south-west and is bordered by a flat area of salt-marsh which provides a safe habitat for many birds, particularly waders, including the tiny, gregarious knot knot whose name is said to derive from Cnut, or Canute, from its habit of running along the tideline. The rare little tern is also to be found here, and you can hear the haunting pipe of the ubiquitous oystercatcher. The shores of the Wash are breathtakingly beautiful in the quiet of a summer sunset, a combination of half-land, half-sea as salt-marsh and sandbank merge. Home of waders, gulls and other birds, seals too are frequent visitors. Occasional schools of pilot whales become embayed, confused by the fierce tides that run in this last vestige of the swamps of the Fens. Before Dutch engineers canalized the rivers and drained the once-malarial marshes in the eighteenth century, these were lawless and wild regions where Hereward the Wake led Saxon resistance against the Norman invader for many years. At the mouth of the Ouse is King's Lynn. King John granted a charter to the town of Lynn, a prosperous port even in the twelfth century and Henry VIII changed its name to King's Lynn when he revised the charter in 1537. Lynn's rival on the northern shore of the Wash is Boston. Like Lynn, it retains a Georgian flavour, reflecting the agricultural wealth of its

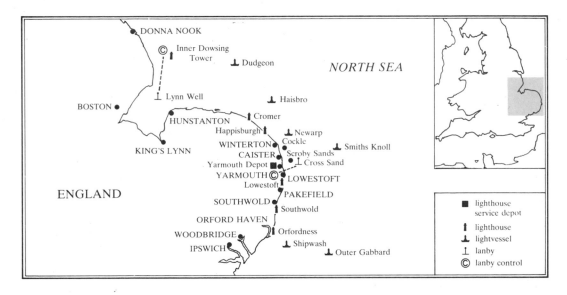

hinterland and remains in operation as a port, despite the recession, partly because the European Economic Community has given a much-needed fillip to its trade. Boston is dominated by its tall church tower, the Boston Stump, which can be seen many miles away and which used to show a lantern to guide travellers. To maintain Boston's connection with the sea, a Grand Sluice was opened in 1766 and an almost continuous process of dredging has gone on ever since. The first dissenters to emigrate in search of religious freedom left from Boston in 1607. They were betrayed and brought back to become a "spectacle and wonder" to the populace who flocked to see them in prison. They later escaped to Leyden in the Netherlands and finally formed part of the contingent who sailed in the *Mayflower* in 1620.

A much-neglected hero who grew up in the shadow of the Boston Stump was Matthew Flinders. At the age of fifteen he joined the Royal Navy during the year of the French Revolution (1789). He served as a midshipman at the battle known as the Glorious First of June on board the 74-gun line-of-battleship *Bellerophon*, the same ship on which Napoleon surrendered over two decades later. He had already attracted some notice for his abilities and under the patronage of Sir Joseph Banks he was engaged for four years under Captain William Bligh (of *Bounty* mutiny fame) in surveying the Australian and Tasmanian coasts. At the close of the century he was promoted, the second youngest captain on the Navy List, and put in command of HMS *Investigator*, sailing from Spithead in July 1801 armed with passports from Bonaparte himself, despite the war between England and France. *Investigator* reached Cape Leeuwin on the south-west corner of Australia in November and began working along the south coast. As a young officer under Bligh and with his friend and fellow townsman, the surgeon's mate, George Bass, Flinders made a remarkable series of small-boat voyages on the Australian coast. He went on to survey much of the Great Barrier Reef and completed the circumnavigation of Australia after many hardships. In addition to his hydrographic work on board the *Investigator*, Flinders also made valuable contributions to the understanding of magnetism, particularly regarding the effects of the earth's field upon a ship's compass. Besides a number of Australian places that bear his name, the vertical bar set before a modern magnetic compass to compensate for the vertical soft iron in a ship's hull is called a Flinder's bar. He left *Investigator* undergoing a refit and sailed for England in the *Porpoise* which was almost immediately wrecked on a sandbank. Flinders took a few men back to Port Jackson in one of the ship's boats and obtained relief for the remainder. Leaving a second time in the *Cumberland*, he put in at the French-held island of Mauritius where he found the authorities would not accept his passport as it was made out for the *Investigator*. For seven years Flinders rotted, a prisoner in a Mauritian gaol. In June 1810 orders for his release at last came through and he arrived in England in October. He found an Admiralty indifferent to his achievements and died in poverty four years later, on 19 July 1814, ironically on the day his narrative, *A Voyage to Terra Australis*, was published. Overshadowed by the events of the great war, Flinders's name is not coupled with deeds of martial daring, although he showed as much courage as any other naval officer of the period. He is almost forgotten in his native land, but deservedly is better remembered in Australia.

Like the coast of Lincolnshire, that of Norfolk hides behind many square miles of shallows. At Hunstanton lights were burned for the benefit of mariners from the lancet windows of a small church dedicated to the Saxon Martyr, King Edmund, who supposedly landed here. In 1665 a pair of leading lights was erected to guide ships through the maze of sandbanks in the Wash, reduced to a single light in 1750. After the remaining high light was destroyed by fire in 1777, its replacement a year later boasted a remarkably efficient optic, designed by Ezekiel Walker of King's Lynn, one of those incomparable, many-sided men of talent produced by the eighteenth century. At once philosopher, scientist and inventor, an academic yet not contemptuous of practical skills, Walker produced numerous papers, including one designed to establish a scale for comparing the brilliance of lights. Impressed by William Hutchinson's reflectors fitted to the new lighthouses erected on the Mersey, Walker constructed reflectors from copper parabolas lined with silver. The concept of setting the light source at the focal centre of a parabola to concentrate the radiating light horizontally was, as we have seen, known as the catoptric system.

In 1828 Trinity House established a lightvessel in the Wash and, after the Act of 1836, acquired the Hunstanton light, rebuilding it in 1840. Subsequently modernized, the light was abandoned in 1921, although most of the tower remains to this day. At Hunstanton the low cliffs have the layered appearance of chocolate gateaux where brown sandstone is topped by thin chalk, with a line of red chalk between them. East of Hunstanton the coast falls away to low salt-marsh. The series of ancient ports from which men once traded and fished are now largely silted. Brancaster, Burnham Overy Staithe and Wells have been badly affected by these deposits, not all of them caused by nature. In the eighteenth century the experimental agriculturalist, Thomas William Coke of nearby Holkham Hall, together with his father, engaged in extensive land-reclamation on the Norfolk coast. This disturbed the natural flow of the tides and destroyed much of their ability to carry silt to sea with the result that the depth of the channels leading to the sea was drastically reduced – the kiss of death to ports already hampered by opening on to a vast area of shallow water.

Coke of Holkham is of interest not only as an eighteenth-century ex-perimentalist, but also as the owner of Dungeness lighthouse in Kent, from which he derived a substantial income. Nevertheless, pride of place on this section of the coast must be yielded to Norfolk's most famous son, for a few miles inland from Burnham Overy Staithe lies the rectory of Burnham Thorpe, birthplace of Horace Nelson. The weak boy who grew to be Vice-Admiral Horatio, Viscount Nelson of the Nile and Duke of Bronte in Sicily, has inspired successive genera-tions and imbued the Royal Navy with an extraordinary spirit. It is odd how a nation which in its imperial heyday admired phlegmatic impassivity as a heroic virtue should have taken such a demonstrative character to its heart but Nelson's abilities, his dedication and his ultimate self-sacrifice mark him as one of our greatest naval heroes.

East of Blakeney, deep water again approaches the coast and only the drowned lands of Foulness extend seawards to any appreciable extent. At the time of the Domesday Book, Cromer stood three miles south of Shipden, a town nestling beneath the headland of Foulness. By the end of the fourteenth century, Shipden had been abandoned and Foulness eroded. All along this section of the coast erosion is caused more by rain and the passage of water horizontally through the clay than by the action of the sea. The water reduces the clay to slime which moves easily and washes itself away. Drying only parches the earth, opening cracks which facilitate the penetration of water at the next downpour. As cliff falls occur, the resultant spoil is swiftly carried away by the sweeping action of the tides. At the time of the Armada scare Foulness was so prominent that it

The Inner Dowsing lighthouse, marking the easternmost extent of the shoals off the Lincolnshire coast, is converted from a former prospecting rig. Oil rigs are a familiar sight in the North Sea and constitute an additional hazard for shipping.

The lighthouse at Southwold is surrounded by the houses and cottages of this delightful little Suffolk town. Opposite top: The grey skies of the North Sea are constantly changing and often dramatic. Centre: Margate, on the north Kent coast has been a popular resort for over two hundred years. Bottom: The busy port of Harwich is one of the two natural harbours on the east coast. It is here that Trinity House maintains its main depot, buoy-yard and Operations Control Centre.

The setting sun in the Thames Estuary casts a sequence of changing light over the grey water.

was made a beacon site, but by the end of the nineteenth century it had vanished. Today its extremity, a shoal patch extending seawards, is marked by a lighted buoy.

Cromer was one of the sites chosen by Sir John Clayton when he made his recommendations for the most suitable sites for lighthouses. We know very little about Clayton; why he was knighted or why he attracted the notice of Charles II – only that he was forever badgering Trinity House with advice. The sites he selected were all sensible and furthermore he obtained widespread support. With his ship-master, George Blake, as a partner, he became a thorn in the flesh of Trinity House, although one of the Corporation's secretaries smugly claimed that Trinity House had succeeded in damning every scheme they had put forward! In 1675 Clayton lit his tower further south at Corton before obtaining permission and came up against no less a person than Samuel Pepys, acting in his capacity as Master of Trinity House. Pepys was opposed to Clayton's growing monopoly and ordered improvements to the Corporation's own light at Lowestoft, declaring the provision of this light free of dues and thus compromising Clayton's tower at Corton. The tower Clayton had completed on Foulness in 1676 was never lit for the same reason. The need for it, however, persisted and in 1719 George I issued letters patent to Nathaniel Life, landowner, and Edward Bowell, merchant, for the building of a lighthouse on Foulness and an octagonal brick tower with an enclosed coal fire was built well inland of Clayton's old tower. In 1792 argand burners and reflectors were fitted and incorporated a revolving apparatus. When Trinity House took over in 1822 these were attended by a man and his two spinster daughters.

Meanwhile the dissolution of Foulness continued. There were landslips in 1799, 1825, 1832 and 1852. In June 1833, with the cliff edge encroaching, the light was abandoned and a new one erected 400 yards inland which, unlike most east coast lighthouses, is made not of brick, but of solid masonry. The speed with which the new tower was built and its appearance suggest the stones were ready prepared for a tower on the west coast. Mr Neville Long sets out the evidence for this theory convincingly in his book the *Lights of East Anglia*. Ironically, Cromer's light, situated on the generally low coast of East Anglia is, at 84 metres above mean sea-level, one of the highest in England, an indication of Foulness's former prominence.

In the autumn of 1866 prolonged rainfall resulted in heavy cliff falls during which the old tower disappeared. The stone tower behind remains, and has been improved as technology provides better equipment. In 1905 a spur was taken off the town's gas supply and provided a brilliant light. Thirty years later a formidable mixture of gas and electricity was used. Today the station is all electric, providing a radio beacon service and a helipad from which relief crews and technicians are flown out to the lightvessels and Inner Dowsing lighthouse to the north. The lighthouse is run by a married keeper.

Cromer is also the home of one of the best known lifeboats on the coast.

From 1909 to 1947 its coxswain was Henry Blogg, a man who became a legend in his own lifetime. His boat is said to have saved no less than 450 lives during the Second World War when the east coast became known as "E-boat Alley". His most spectacular rescue was of the crew of the sailing barge *Sepoy*, aground in the breakers off Cromer during an onshore gale. There was scarcely water to float a cockle-shell but her crew could be seen from the beach, clinging to her rigging.

The relief of the Smith Knoll lightvessel, off the Norfolk coast.

No help could reach them through the violent surf so Blogg sailed his lifeboat on to *Sepoy*'s hatch on one sea, picked up the survivors in the trough, and coolly allowed himself to be swept off on the succeeding wave!

Between Cromer and Hemsby the cliffs level out to a coast of sand dunes and groynes. Vast sums are spent annually to maintain the sea-defences here and slow the southward scour of the tide. From seaward the land is marked by the handsome flint towers of Norfolk's lovely churches. But for all its mild beauty, this stretch of coast rivals the Goodwins in terms of swallowing ships and sailors. Two passages exist off Yarmouth, both lie inside the main banks of the Newarp and Smith's Knoll. The offshore passage lies to seaward of the Scroby Sands, past the Cross Sand and then south to Orfordness. An inshore passage, through a gap in the sands called the Cockle Gat, leads through the shoals past Great Yarmouth and Lowestoft, offering some shelter from the prevailing winds. This meant a convergence of shipping off the Cockle Gat, particularly in the days of the great sailing trade between the Tyne and London. During the sixteenth and seventeenth centuries Wintertonness, like Foulness, extended seawards to constrict the entrance and disasters were frequent. In bad weather in a single day in 1592 fifty ships foundered off it. In 1692 a thousand seamen were estimated to have perished in a night, and on 30 October 1789 two convoys of merchantmen ran foul of each other as one sailed north, the other south. In the ensuing chaos twenty-three ships foundered, twenty ran ashore and six hundred seamen died.

In 1600 Trinity House had established two candle lighthouses at Caister, near Yarmouth, under their own management. A few years later, after an extensive survey of the shoals off Yarmouth, the Elder Brethren established another pair of lights at Lowestoft, upon the ness, the most easterly point in England, to direct ships "which crept by night in the dangerous passage betwixt Lowestoft and Winterton". At about this time the first Trinity House buoys were laid around the off-lying shoals and the first buoy-yachts based at Yarmouth. In 1616 two Elder Brethren selected sites for lights at the other end of the passage at Wintertonness. At the same time our old and gallant friend John Meldrum (who was to die at the siege of Scarborough) also obtained a patent to erect lights at Winterton. The case of Trinity House against Meldrum was brought before the Privy Council and its ramifications are complex. Trinity House justified its delays by pointing to constant shifting of the channels, but this of course did not prevent the disasters that occurred every winter. The reliability of leading lights depended upon the stability of the channel, otherwise they simply became "misleading lights". Concluding their case, the Brethren pointed out that Meldrum was no seaman and that no one was more qualified than they to decide the point; "else," they said "let us suffer to be hanged at the gates of the King's court for example to others".

But Meldrum pleaded his case plausibly and won. He was afterwards successful in obtaining patents for lights on Orfordness and the North and South Forelands. In 1677, after a series of violent storms, the Cockle Gat altered and Trinity House added a low light to the original private light at Winterton to provide a new lead through the channel. This additional pair of lights had to be moved several times but it can scarcely have given much comfort for a stranger approaching the coast to discover, as Defoe did in 1722, that Wintertonness boasted two pairs of leading lights. This thoroughly confusing situation existed until the disaster of October 1789 when the public outcry (complicated by the existence of yet another pair of lights a few miles south at Caister!) forced the reduction of Winterton lights to one, the erection of a better pair of leading lights a few miles away at Happisburgh and the suppression of the Caister lights. Winterton continued to show a steady light until it was discontinued in 1921. The tower was sold as a private house but continues to provide a service to the mariner by having a racon mounted on it. In 1843 a lightvessel was moored to mark the Cockle Gat. It has now been replaced by a buoy of the largest class. In 1883 the front light at Happisburgh was demolished and the rear light altered to a flashing "passage" light that still functions.

The shoals that cause all this trouble extend from Winterton southwards past Great Yarmouth to Benacre Ness, five miles beyond Lowestoft. They are constantly shifting, although they may assume a stable character for some years before a sudden and unpredictable movement like a gigantic and irresistible convulsion. Indeed one of the fascinations of this coast is the comparative modernity of these movements. Backed by the Broads, Great Yarmouth is founded on one of those tide-transported sand-spits, known as "shingle forelands" that have been carried down from the north. Much of Yarmouth is probably built on the foundations of Foulness and the ancient town of Shipden. Breydon Water was once a tidal river estuary which became closed off by the sand and left to "pond back". The great Romano-British fort at Burgh Castle is evidence that Breydon was once open directly to the sea and not diverted by the isthmus upon which Yarmouth now stands. Similar havens exist further south. Until the land begins to rise again south of Yarmouth piers, the coast is low-lying, the skyline stabbed by the power station chimneys, the pylons, buildings, the ferris wheel and the monument to Nelson. Atop the column, Britannia stares inland, a direction, it is said, that the sculptor did not intend and which supposedly drove him to suicide. It was at Yarmouth that Nelson landed after an overland journey from Naples, via Austria and Germany, following his annihilation of the French fleet in Abukir Bay. At Yarmouth too, he had his classic row with Admiral Sir Hyde Parker some two years later, before the fleet sailed for Denmark and Nelson snatched victory from potential disaster at Copenhagen on Easter Sunday, 1801.

A fine anchorage with good holding ground, Yarmouth Roads was the main harbour throughout the Napoleonic Wars for the squadron that bottled up the Dutch fleet in the Texel, a hundred miles to the east. In 1797, when the great naval mutinies broke out, the North Sea squadron was commanded by the Scotsman, Adam Duncan. Immobilized by the mutiny, Duncan nonetheless managed to keep the Dutch in port by stationing a handful of small and loyal ships off the Texel which signalled frequently to what Duncan hoped the Dutch would assume to be the main British fleet just over the horizon. Duncan meanwhile was coping with the mutiny. When the crew of his own flagship defied him, the huge admiral waded among them and, picking up one of the ring leaders by the scruff of his neck, held him over the ship's side. "This fellow seeks to deprive me of the command of the ship!" he boomed, and this act defused the situation. After a rise in pay and promises of reform, his squadron sailed off to destroy the Dutch fleet off Camperdown.

Although Trinity House kept, and continues to keep, a wary eye upon the shifting sandbanks off Yarmouth and Lowestoft, full surveying is undertaken by the Hydrographic Department of the Royal Navy. One of the first officers to carry out the original complete survey of the southern North Sea was Captain

Hewitt. Hewitt gave his name to the new channel that appeared about 1838, replacing the St Nicholas Gat that had led out of Yarmouth Roads to the east. But in 1982 the Hewitt Channel in turn suddenly filled in and the tides carved out the present fairway through the Corton Channel. Hewitt himself was lost in November 1840 when his survey vessel, HMS *Fairy*, foundered with all hands off the Suffolk coast during a fierce gale.

Great Yarmouth was famous for its herring for over thirteen hundred years. Before the Norman Conquest "Angles, French and Belgians" had a fishing settlement at the mouth of the Yare, and as early as 647 AD a church was built at Great Yarmouth dedicated to St Nicholas, the patron saint of fishermen. The fishery was seasonal until the coming of the steam drifter and the technical advances in fishing during the last sixty or seventy years. In the first decade of the present century the herring trade enjoyed a phenomenal boom but this has resulted in an almost total exhaustion of the North Sea stock and hardly a herring is landed today at Great Yarmouth. It is quite likely that what has happened to the herring as a food source will happen to other species elsewhere in due course.

For about four hundred years Great Yarmouth throve on the herring fishery, from the Middle Ages to the mid-1960s. So important was it to the economy of the town that when, on one occasion, the southward drift of shingle almost choked the entrance to the port, the townsfolk turned out in force to dig it away by hand and so preserve the means by which the town prospered. Today the offshore gas and oil industries have injected new life into the port, as has our joining the European Economic Community, reviving a short-sea trade with our Dutch neighbours.

Today Yarmouth is a holiday maker's paradise, and to the south, where low cliffs front the old village of Corton, summer sunshine glints off hundreds of caravan roofs. The land remains high as it stretches southwards towards Lowestoft and the ness that is the most easterly part of England. Lowestoft Ness fronts the higher land and it was on this low foreshore that the town of Lowestoft had its first origins as a fishing centre. The town was reached up steep paths, or "scores", but its importance as a port was due to the inlet known as Lake Lothing, fed by the meandering River Waveney. The main fairway through the shoals was known as the Standforth, a beautifully picturesque name, regrettably corrupted to Stanford. This channel has long since disappeared and the main approach is now through Yarmouth Roads, via the Cockle Gat or the new Corton Channel, after which ships work south inshore. A shallow tidal channel does exist to the southward, through Pakefield Road, but it is not much used. Fishing is still carried out from Lowestoft, but on a much reduced scale. The height of the herring boom around 1912 supported 700 drifters, mostly steam-powered, which landed their catch to be sent by rail to London's Billingsgate market. Many of these steam fishing vessels did yeoman service during both World Wars, serving a variety of roles. Today herring forms only a minor part of the catch and it is mostly plaice, dogfish, cod and other species that are landed here.

Trinity House's connection with Lowestoft began as early as 1609 when it owned a pair of leading lights to guide ships in through the Standforth Channel. We have already seen how the improvements to these were undertaken as much to defeat Sir John Clayton as to aid navigation. The result of the dispute was the fine tower built during the Mastership of Samuel Pepys in 1676 and the arms of Pepys may still be seen today alongside those of the Corporation. When the rebuilding was finished, mariners were informed that the new high lighthouse would be a fire light, rather than a candle light, but after two town fires the Elder Brethren enclosed the grate in a lantern for fear of being responsible for a third. In the 1680s two keepers were employed at £30 after a year's satisfactory service.

In 1706 the low light on the foreshore was discontinued but protests soon caused a new one to be provided in 1730. It was built so that it might be moved as the Standforth Channel shifted, maintaining an accurate transit through the shoals. On Christmas Eve 1739 a great gale blew up, destroying the town of Dunwich a few miles to the south, and driving sixteen ships ashore at Lowestoft. Again, in December 1757, twenty-two ships drove ashore, and in December 1770 a further thirty were wrecked or stranded between Yarmouth and Southwold. On Lowestoft beach alone eighteen were cast up at dawn and by noon a dozen had been smashed to pieces. Although these losses cannot be directly attributed to poor lights, Trinity House were at some pains to make Lowestoft lighthouse a major aid to navigation on the coast rather than just a local lead through the banks. In 1778 a new "spangle light" was unveiled. This comprised a waisted drum, rather like a large cotton reel, to which were glued 4,000 small squares of mirrored glass which reflected the light from a central ring of 126 oil lamp-wicks. The light was first observed by Mr Allison Davie, the local Trinity House agent responsible for the buoyage around the offshore banks. Later the Elder Brethren arrived in their splendidly ornate and gilded cutter to see the wonderful new light for themselves. The flickering quality of the flames reflected off the slight irregularities of the glass facets gave the light its name and made it visible on a clear, dark night from more than twenty miles. However, Argand's improvements soon rendered the spangle light obsolete and in 1796 it was replaced. But some thirty years later there were still complaints that many of the town's house lights were brighter. The Trinity House agent was sent to sea to investigate and, as a result of his report, the people of Lowestoft were circulated with handbills asking them to draw their curtains at night!

The approaches to the port continued to be bedevilled by constant changes in depth and a series of subsidiary lighthouses was built. One at Pakefield was lit on May Day 1832 and put in the charge of a retired shipmaster, "late of the Jamaica trade". The light was discontinued in 1864 when the channels shifted again, but the tower remains part of a holiday camp. At this time another light was set up at Kessingland, only to share the same fate. A pair of leading lights built at Hopton were of use for only six years and were demolished in 1871.

The problem of providing a leading line through the approach channel continued to exercise the ingenuity of Trinity House engineers well into the last century. In 1867 James Douglass, the chief civil engineer employed by the Corporation, of whom we shall hear more, replaced the old low light down on the foreshore with a handsome wrought-iron structure that was capable of being re-sited without undue trouble. Following this advance, it was decided to modify the high light and to install electric power. On completion of the building work,

The lighthouse at Lowestoft as it is today.

the new paraffin lights then coming into service were found to be so efficient that one was installed and, at long last, combined with a flashing apparatus. Electricity was finally connected in 1936 and since 1974 the station has been fully automatic.

Douglass's low light was moved to a new location shortly after it was made occulting, but this did not save the keepers' dwellings which were soon engulfed by the sea. As a result, the light was made automatic and moved further inland again in 1894. Effective sea defences were also erected to protect the ness. However these caused severe erosion to the south, almost entirely destroying Pakefield village, and led to severe changes in the tidal flow offshore. The Standforth Channel ceased to exist and with it the need to maintain Lowestoft lights as leading marks. The lower light was, therefore, extinguished for the last time at daybreak on 27 August 1923 and the wrought-iron structure taken down. The main light was left on the cliff above.

The coast protrudes again five miles south of Lowestoft at Benacre Ness, a shingle headland off which lies the last of the banks and shoals that make the approaches to Lowestoft and Great Yarmouth so dangerous. The sweep of the tides here is fast and the water rolls tons of spoil southwards to the great shingle forelands of Orfordness and Landguard Point. It is this carriage of silt that has almost entirely closed the River Blythe at Walberswick, and choked up the adjacent entrance to Buss Creek where once herring busses discharged their cargoes of fish at Southwold. These neighbouring waterways once formed entries to Blythburgh, Southwold, Walberswick and Dunwich and their disappearance gave rise to the doggerel verse:

> Southwold and Dunwich and Walberswick
> All go in at one lousy creek.

The wealthy medieval port of Dunwich was probably founded in Romano-British times. By the seventh century it was the capital of East Anglia and the seat of a bishop. It boasted a college which, some claim, was the origin of Cambridge University. King John granted the town a charter and it provided Edward I with eleven ships of war. But Dunwich was soon under attack by the sea. In 1347 more than 400 of its houses were washed away after a storm and again, in 1570, more damage resulted in an appeal to Elizabeth I. The great gale of Christmas Eve 1739 effectively destroyed what remained of the town, although it continued to return two Members of Parliament until the Reform Act of 1832. It was during the second decade of the present century that the disappearance of the parish church finally occurred. All that remains are local stories of the church bells tolling in a storm.

Today neighbouring Southwold is the most prosperous remainder of these little towns. Once a fishing port of note, Southwold was provided with cannon by Charles I to defend itself against the depredations of the French corsairs from Dunkirk. These were replaced in 1745 and remained on Gun Hill for many years although during the two World Wars these ancient weapons were removed and hidden away, a classic instance of bureaucratic logic. Today they have been reinstated and I remember when I was a boy, standing beside one, watching one of the last sprit-rigged sailing barges making a passage offshore with a cargo. Southwold lighthouse stands pristine and white in the centre of the town and is the highest point for many miles. The need for a light at Southwold arose from severe erosion at Orfordness to the south which threatened the lighthouses there. A temporary structure was put up at Southwold in 1887 and was then replaced by the handsome lighthouse which stands today near Adnams' Brewery. It was first lit in February 1889.

The shallow bay upon which Southwold stands is known as Solebay and gave

The Isle of Portland is joined to the mainland by the south-eastern tip of Chesil Beach. The lighthouse on Portland Bill used to be the tallest in the Service until the present tower was built at Dungeness.

Looking towards Calshot Power Station, at the mouth of Southampton Water.

Below top: The six miles of quay at the head of Southampton water made it one of the busiest waterways in Britain before the recession. Centre: The view in the sheltered waters of the Solent, just outside the entrance to Southampton Water. Bottom: The Nab Tower marks the eastern end of the Solent.

its name to a seventeenth-century battle against the Dutch. The British fleet under the command of King Charles II's brother James, Duke of York (afterwards James II), was in an unusual alliance with a French squadron under D'Estrées. This combined fleet lay at anchor off Southwold on 28 May 1672, taking in fresh provisions, when the Dutch, under De Ruyter, descended on them with a favourable wind. The two English divisions got under way with some difficulty and stood north, leaving the less experienced French to be cut off by part of De Ruyter's fleet. The Dutch Admiral then concentrated his main power on the English ships and a bloody battle ensued which included an attack by Dutch fireships. Several vessels on both sides blew up, and the action was so fierce that the Duke of York was obliged to shift his flag three times before eventually the Dutch drew off.

Today, where once the battle pennons of the three fleets streamed from opposing mastheads, one may be lucky enough to see a skein of geese, or a flight of Whooper swans heading for the bird reserve at Minsmere, lying behind the low cliffs that sweep southwards from Walberswick. If you are more than fortunate, you may spot marsh harriers or avocets which returned to East Anglia during the Second World War when the area was closed to the public.

Dominating the southern end of Solebay, the huge, ugly, boxlike mass of the Sizewell power stations squat, glowing sinisterly by night and steaming quietly by day. Offshore, two concrete structures mark the intakes and outfalls of the cooling water. Some 27 million gallons of seawater an hour are required to cool the reactor in Sizewell A alone. Another quantitive record was set here in the eighteenth century, when smugglers landed 8,000 gallons of good Hollands gin on the beach at Sizewell during the course of a single night.

Rounding Thorpeness to the south of Sizewell, one sees two conspicuous buildings above the trees. One is known as "the house in the clouds", a water tower disguised as an elevated house; the second is a windmill, transported here from another location. Closer inspection ashore reveals a number of architectural wonders, all the result of the imagination of the author, Glencairn Stuart Ogilvie, who laid out this holiday village before the First World War. A mile south of Thorpeness, Aldeburgh's seafront is attractive from the sea, with its Georgian houses and medieval Moot Hall, its lifeboat slip on the shingle, its church tower and, to the south of the town, the Martello tower. One of the largest of these anti-Napoleonic fortifications, Aldeburgh's tower is the first in a long chain round the vulnerable south-east coast where, it was feared, Napoleon's veterans might land. Based on the design of a round tower which resisted British troops at Mortella in Corsica, the towers were intended as lookout points with a small garrison and a single gun to sweep the beaches with grapeshot. South of Aldeburgh the towers are extremely frequent and, although surrounded by modern buildings, easily identified. Within a few yards of the Martello tower, the River Alde heads doggedly towards the sea, but it is then deflected southwards by Sudborne Beach, a rampart of shingle constantly reinforced by the southern movement of spoil. The river ponds back, swings through a right angle and changes its name to the River Ore. It then runs south-west, behind Orfordness, past the town of Orford and emerges many miles to the south at North Weir Point.

Orford is a delightful town, with an ancient church and an impressive Norman castle. The keep of the castle, conspicuous from the sea, is unique, having an octagonal outer section, buttressed by three square towers and a low gatehouse, while its inner section is circular. Built by Henry II between 1166 and 1172, in 1217, during the Baron's War against King John it was occupied by the French. In 1336 Edward III gave it to Robert Ufford, Earl of Suffolk and it remained in private hands until 1962. At the height of Orford's prosperity as a port during the Middle Ages, the river debouched into the sea opposite its quays. Today this happens some four miles further south. Recent studies of the spit reveal that the movement of shingle is not constant. For long periods the extremity, or distal point, remains stationary (as it did for many years during Orford's boom period). Occasionally the southward growth of the shingle is reversed, the spit severed, its extremity is washed away and a new distal point forms. Orfordness itself is the knuckle upon this long shingle foreland where the coast suddenly swings south-west and is usually considered to mark the northern limit of the Thames Estuary.

The drift of shingle along the coast also has its effect offshore. During the seventeenth century, coincident with the progressive destruction of Foulness and Wintertonness, changes occurred in the seabed off Orfordness. Negotiating the headland at Orford was complicated by growing shoals and the powerful coal-merchants lobbied Trinity House for lights. Nothing was done until 28 October 1627 when, once again, bad weather decimated shipping. A fleet of colliers was caught off Aldeburgh, several struck the Aldeburgh Napes (a bank just off the town) while others were swept south on to the Shipwash Sand. Thirty-two were driven ashore on Orfordness where their crews perished almost to a man.

A new petition was submitted. It went to Trinity House and then to the Privy Council where it languished for several years. Meanwhile John Meldrum who, it will be recollected, had succeeded in obtaining sanction to erect lights at Winterton in the teeth of opposition from Trinity House, decided to seize the initiative. Meldrum's petition to Charles I declared that he would take no more than one penny a ton as dues, and would exempt fishermen and colliers. At this time Meldrum, who appears to have come from Scotland in the entourage of James I, enjoyed the royal favour of James's son, Charles I, and was granted leave to build "two temporary lighthouses to lead between Sizewell Bank and Aldeburgh Napes to the north". I have already mentioned that he soon disposed of his East Anglian lighthouses in favour of ownership of the North and South Forelands in Kent, but, for a while, he was the greatest lighthouse proprietor in the land.

Meldrum's successor at Aldeburgh was Alderman Gore who apparently constructed the towers of timber. The high light showed a coal fire; the low, a candle light. The death of one of the keepers resulted in the appointment of his widow, although Gore later regretted this: "I have had more complaints in this half-year than ever I had in your father or your husband's time. I did not think you would have been so careless but I excuse it because you are a woman," he wrote. Ironically, the lights passed to Gore's daughter Sarah on his own death and then, upon her marriage, to her husband, Edward Turnour. Sadly Sarah did not make old bones and died leaving a large family. Turnour, a lawyer, did well (as lawyers are wont to do) and earned a knighthood at the Restoration. He was elected MP for Hertford in 1661 and chosen as Speaker of the House of Commons. He was influential enough to obtain an extension of the original lease for the lighthouses as "a personal reward for services to the Crown". Turnour went on to become Solicitor-General and Lord Chief Baron of the Exchequer, soon after which he died. His son promptly wasted the family fortune at Charles II's frivolous court.

The remoteness of the Orfordness lights made them difficult to supervise and complaints constantly arrived at Trinity House. Such excuses as "the east wind makes the sea darken the light" were put up by the keepers and believed by the owners. The proprietorship of lighthouses now being fashionable, leases were bought and sold and Turnour Junior lost control. One Ralph Grey petitioned for ownership and a tedious legal battle began.

Meanwhile, on the lonely shingle strand one keeper had been carried off by a press-gang while the encroachment of the sea had carried away the front light itself. In 1700 the coasting trade refused further dues and Trinity House decided it was time to act. A clerk named Samuel Hunter produced a damning report, so improvements were made and in 1702 a party of Elder Brethren arrived to inspect the results. Soon, though, there was a new hazard when in June 1707 French privateers landed, attacked the lights and made off with the keepers' bedding. The following year, disdaining to land for such paltry pickings, a privateer "did shoote at the Lithouse and have Broke all the glass".

Two years later the sea carried away the second front light and in 1720 the ownership dispute was at last settled in favour of Grey, although Turnour's men were still in possession of the lights and when Grey arrived at Orford he was refused the keys. Towards sunset Grey, his agent and keepers approached the lighthouse for the second time, and after a scuffle, evicted the former occupants. Grey soon replaced the ramshackle timber-work with two brick towers at a cost of £1,850, but the sea continued to erode the coast and in 1724 the front light again disappeared. Grey sensibly replaced it with a structure that was movable. By this time, however, he was in financial trouble and leaving a suicide note, he vanished, only to reappear after being pronounced dead by the House of Commons. His private coffers must have been replenished for, when the front light was again washed away, it was replaced by a new, oil-fuelled structure in the following spring. Alas, the keepers were not able to handle this innovation and the light caught fire, as did its successor! The action of the sea upon the ness must have altered abruptly for the second replacement stood for sixty years.

After Grey's death, ownership of Orfordness and Wintertonness lights passed, via his wife, to John Griffin, later 1st Baron Braybrooke, who owned the lights from 1762 until 1797 when the enormous profits made by some owners were attracting hostile criticism. Braybrooke's heir died soon after inheriting the title and the 3rd Lord Braybrooke found it necessary to renew the lease. By a coincidence he was also the decipherer of Pepys's diaries and therefore in a position to omit all the comments about the private ownership of lighthouses, which Pepys, as Master of Trinity House, had sedulously opposed, losing his seat in Parliament as MP for Harwich as a consequence. In the course of the negotiations for the lease, Braybrooke revealed that a net sum of £13,414 had been derived from the lights at Winterton and Orford. Braybrooke was not long in possession of his lighthouses, losing them after the passing of the Act of 1836.

While these changes had been occurring in the ownership, certain alterations had again taken place at Orfordness. After a period of comparative stability, a gale blew up in October 1789 and left the front light at the water's edge. The distance between the high and low lights had now become too short to form an effective transit and the former front light was abandoned, the rear light converted to a front light and a new high light built behind it. This was nearly ninety feet tall, oil-fuelled and fitted with argand burners and reflectors. These alterations were completed by 1793, four years before the death of the 1st Lord Braybrooke.

The shoreline remained fairly static for almost a century until in 1887 another gale breached the shingle and again left the low light teetering on the sea's edge. This led to the building of Southwold lighthouse. As a result of the loss of the low light, Orfordness was abandoned as a leading light station. The lighthouse was fitted with a flashing light, becoming, with neighbouring Southwold, Lowestoft and the whole chain of lighthouses around the curve of the coast of East Anglia, a "beacon light", showing a characteristic flash seawards from which passing vessels could derive a compass bearing. Today the station is fully automatic, the most powerful lighthouse on the coast. The arms of Lord Braybrooke are still visible over the doorway, although the flanking keepers' dwellings have been demolished. The red-banded white tower stands solitary upon the great shingle promontory as the North Sea nibbles ever closer, and the roar of pebbles may be heard in the waves that break upon its tideline and the flood sweeps southwards into the Thames Estuary.

CHAPTER FOUR

ESTUARY AND STRAIT

North Foreland.

From Orfordness to the North Foreland in Kent, the estuary of the Thames is some forty miles wide. It is seamed with alternating sandbanks and channels for it is the meeting place of two tidal streams and the fresh-water not only out of the Thames but also of the other rivers that share the estuary – the Medway, Crouch, Blackwater and Colne. These all affect the disposition of the shoals and fairways, but it is the two tidal streams whose impact is greatest. The North Sea stream, which we have seen carrying the spoil of wasted headlands south along the East Anglian littoral, floods into the Thames from the north-eastward, influencing the lie of both shoals and the deeper water between them. From the opposite direction the Channel flood sweeps up from the Dover Strait around the North Foreland and into the estuary over the less well-defined and shallower flats off north Kent. Much of the energy of the Channel tide is expended along the coasts of the Low Countries, so it is the scour of the North Sea tides in both ebb and flood which have the greater influence on the estuary. The principal fairways into the Thames lie on a north-east/south-west axis, roughly parallel to the Essex coast. The two main channels into the Thames, the Barrow Deep and the Black Deep, both run along this line. The entrances from the south, along the edge of the Kentish Flats are the Prince's and the Edinburgh Channels.

The depth of these fairways has made a natural highway of the estuary, although the drying sandbanks complicate its navigation. As these channels served London directly, Trinity House assumed responsibility for marking them comparatively early. We know that buoys already existed when William of Orange landed in 1688, for an order went out from those loyal to James II that buoys in the Thames were to be destroyed to hamper his approach (although as it turned out, William's landing place was many miles to the west). The present North-East Gunfleet station off Clacton-on-Sea has been buoyed since 1684. Although only twenty-one buoys were in the estuary in 1777, this number had tripled by the end of the Napoleonic War. Unlike Yarmouth where Allison Davie acted as agent for the Corporation, the mouth of the Thames was the direct responsibility of one of the Elder Brethren, known as the Buoy Warden, who directed a small number of buoy-yachts in the ceaseless duty of maintaining the buoys and their moorings. The earliest recorded order was to one of the yacht-masters in 1745 "to go down in the Trinity Sloop to clean the buoys in the South Channel". During the Napoleonic War, Trinity House ordered its buoy-yachts to destroy the seamarks to prevent the mutinous fleet at the Nore from defecting to republican France or Holland. At the conclusion of the mutiny, Trinity House presented the Admiralty with a bill for restitution of the buoyage, rounded to the nearest three pence!

The coastline of the estuary south-west of Orfordness is unrelieved shingle until the Ore meets the sea at North Weir Point. From this point until the Deben's mouth at Bawdsey, low cliffs are backed by woods. The line of Martello towers is almost continuous along this section of coast backing the shallow indentation known as Hollesley Bay. Used as an anchorage by French and Dutch alike, it was from here that the two Dutch leaders, De Ruyter and Evertsen, waited before storming Landguard Fort at the entrance to Harwich Harbour in 1667.

Harwich Harbour shares with the Humber the distinction of being one of the two natural sheltered anchorages on the entire east coast of England. Its approach is difficult, lying behind a number of large offshore shoals such as the Shipwash. Extensive dredging has been carried out for many years, most recently to straighten the channels and increase the depths sufficiently to admit the largest container vessels to Felixstowe's quays. The harbour is formed by the confluence of the Rivers Stour and Orwell. Berths exist at Harwich, Parkeston and Mistley on the Stour, and at Ipswich on the Orwell, as well as at Felixstowe. From Parkeston the ferries serve German, Danish and Dutch ports, while at Harwich Trinity House maintains its principal depot, buoy-yard and Operations Control Centre. The tenders come and go from Harwich pier, loading and discharging buoys and their moorings, picking up lightvessels and light-floats from their moorings in the River Stour, and changing their own crews in the continuous round that makes up the offshore activities of the Corporation.

To the south of Harwich, the land falls back to an area of creeks and salt-marsh which has inspired several authors. Known as the Walton Backwaters, Paul Gallico called it "The Great Marsh" in his book *The Snow Goose*, but it is probably more familiar as the *Secret Water* of one of Arthur Ransome's Swallows and Amazons stories. It is still a favourite spot for yachtsmen, rich in wild-life, and its many creeks and islands are as fascinating today as when Ransome sailed upon its waters in the 1930s. It is almost surrounded by land, being closed in from the east by the hummock of Walton's Naze. The Naze is topped by a brick tower, erected in 1720 as a "daymark" (a conspicuous feature from which to derive a position) by Trinity House and has recently been sold to a private owner. Although shallow water extends to seaward of the Naze, a channel exists close inshore at high tide, surveyed in about 1800 by Graeme Spence, the Admiralty's

Head Maritime Surveyor. In 1801 Nelson was commanding the Anti-Invasion Flotilla, anchored in Harwich Harbour, on board HMS *Medusa*. He received urgent orders to sail without delay for the Nore but he was pinned in Harwich by an easterly wind. On hearing a report that Mr Spence knew of a passage due south, inside the Cork Sand, Nelson sent for him and under his direction *Medusa* took the tide through the channel, which has been known by the ship's name ever since.

From Walton-on-Naze to Point Clear at the mouths of the Colne and the Blackwater, the coast consists of alternating marsh, sand-flats and low cliff. Much of the marsh has been drained and the sea is kept at bay by a series of sea-defences. The Blackwater is proving a favourite laying-up anchorage for redundant shipping during the present recession, while the River Crouch is still used by commercial ships as well as by myriads of yachtsmen who have made Burnham-on-Crouch the Cowes of the east coast. South of the Crouch, a vast area of drying sand is visible at low water off the island of Foulness. Known as the Maplin Sands, it has been considered as a possible site for London's third airport, but for the time being it is used as a gunnery range and is the feeding ground for grey-lag and brent geese who manage to co-exist with the artillery shells. Ships bound for the container berths of Tilbury, the oil-discharging points of Grain and Shellhaven, enter the river through the Barrow or Black Deeps. These, and the southern fairways of the Edinburgh and Prince's Channels, all converge at Southend just opposite the point at which the Medway joins the Thames on the southern shore of the estuary.

From Southend, the sea is left behind and the banks close in. Although the tide still invades the river, the habitations of man and the industrial chaos he causes become dominant. Writing of the same place at the height of its prosperity in the late nineteenth century, in *The Mirror of the Sea* Joseph Conrad said,

> Between the crowded houses of Gravesend and the monstrous red-brick pile on the Essex shore the ship is surrendered fairly to the grasp of the river.... The salt, acrid flavour is gone out of the air, together with a sense of unlimited space opening free beyond the threshold of sandbanks below the Nore. The waters of the sea rush on past Gravesend, tumbling the big mooring buoys laid along the face of the town; but the sea-freedom stops short there, surrendering the salt tide to the needs, the artifices, the contrivances of toiling men.

This is a fair description today, though those contrivances extend further seawards and Conrad would now have to employ a more corrosive adjective than "acrid" to describe the discharges of industry.

Behind the Kentish Flats lies the Isle of Sheppey and the unresistant coast of north Kent, subject to much erosion. The chalk headland of the North Foreland stands upon what was once the Isle of Thanet. Reculver marks the northern end of the strait that separated it from the Weald; Richborough, with its great Roman fortress, marks the southern end. Close by Sandwich was once an important Cinque port standing on the (second) River Stour which crawls sluggishly seaward through mudflats into Pegwell Bay. Set on the chalk cliffs, its neighbour Ramsgate continues to enjoy prosperity as a port and the cliffs produce some extraordinary effects from their erosion. Sharp cut bays, or re-entrants, are known locally as "gates" and indicate access to the sea. It was at one of these, known now as Kingsgate, that Charles II landed on his return to England in 1660.

To seaward of the Kentish coast as it swings south round the North Foreland, lie the most notorious sandbanks of them all: the Goodwins. Supposedly named after Earl Godwin (a Saxon noble who was the ancestor of King Harold), who

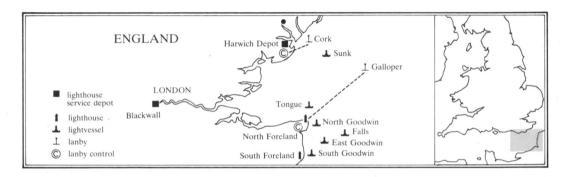

held land in Kent, they have been known to generations of seamen as the "Great Ship Swallower". There is a passage inside the Goodwins that leads directly to the anchorage known as The Downs, off Deal, but the main shipping lane is outside, to the eastwards round the trio of Trinity House lightvessels that mark the extremity of the banks.

The Downs is one of the most historic of English anchorages. For hundreds of years ships requiring a westerly wind to get out of the Thames had to wait here for a favourable slant from the east to get away down channel. It was also a frequent refuge in bad weather and many of the wrecks on the Goodwin Sands have occurred from ships in The Downs driving from their anchors, or from miscalculations by sailors trying to make shelter. Ironically, this anchorage was of such national importance that the need to preserve its security was advanced as an argument *against* building a lighthouse there.

In 1634 Trinity House argued that the expense of a lighthouse would not only be an intolerable burden upon trade and damage the interests of pilots but that "in times of hostility such lights would be a means to light an enemy to land and, in chase by night, ships would be brought to where the King's ships and unarmed merchantmen rode peacefully at anchor and then those pursuing vessels might . . . board the merchantmen . . . True, the lighthouses might be put out, yet they would so far do mischief as to acquaint strangers with the coast . . . " Asked for their opinion, the men of Dover were even more forthright:

We at sea have always marks more certain and sure than lights, high land and soundings that we trust more than lights ... The Goodwins are no more dangerous now than time out of mind they were, and lighthouses would never lull the tempests, the real cause of shipwreck. If lighthouses had been of any service at the Forelands the Trinity House, as guardians of shipping, would have put them there.

That would seem to be conclusive, except that, once again, Sir John Meldrum comes on the scene, obtains a patent and erects wooden light towers at the North and South Forelands. Faced with this *fait accompli*, Trinity House approached the Privy Council and offered to take them over. It is a measure of Meldrum's influence that the Corporation were curtly told once again that their proposal "comes out of time". From this point both sets of lighthouses come under common ownership and their history is inseparable. Meldrum established two towers at the South Foreland (their transit leading clear over the southern extremity of the Goodwin Sands) and a single light at the North Foreland. His first tower at the North Foreland burned down, as did its replacement. Nevertheless he persisted and the coal-fired grates eventually fitted burned about 100 tons a year, the keepers using bellows to keep the fires glowing on windless nights.

Sadly, provision of the lights did not prevent disaster striking the ships anchored in The Downs on the night of 30 November 1703 when the greatest gale ever recorded in England occurred. This was the same wind which caused the fire at Spurn Head to melt the grate bars. For the shipping anchored in The Downs it was catastrophic. Numerous merchantmen were lost, as was the entire fleet of men-of-war under Admiral Beaumont. Of course these wrecks were in reality only the most dramatic of a continuous series of strandings and the establishment of these lights had significantly improved accuracy of navigation.

Meldrum's wooden structures at the two Forelands were replaced about 1719 by octagonal brick towers built by the Admiralty who, regarding The Downs as an anchorage of great importance strategically, had taken over the responsibility themselves. Light dues were used to fund Greenwich Hospital to look after naval seamen "in a decayed or distressed condition". The original lights had glazed-in coal grates but these proved too sooty and so were reopened. In 1792 the towers were remodelled, raised and fitted with argand burners, reflectors and lenses. But lighthouses alone were insufficient and a demand for lightships was made: "the bare interest of the property lost on the Goodwin Sands in one year would maintain a floating light as long as this world continues." The first lightvessel was established at the north end of the Goodwin Sands in 1795, others following at the east and southern points. The Elder Brethren's old objection that "a lightship would not ride, would break adrift and drown all the people" proved tragically true in November 1954 when the South Goodwin lightvessel parted her chain mooring in a ferocious gale, drove on to the sand and rolled over. Only one man escaped, an observer attached to the Ministry of Agriculture and Fisheries.

The Trinity House crew were lost and no trace of their bodies was ever found, the wreck of the lightvessel soon afterwards sinking in the sand.

In 1898 Guglielmo Marconi used South Foreland lighthouse as a base for tests with wireless telegraphy, receiving the first message transmitted over the air from the hand of a Trinity House lightsman on board the East Goodwin light-vessel. A letter in *The Times* explained its use:

> . . . a touch of the key aboard the lightship suffices to ring a bell in a room at South Foreland lighthouse, twelve miles away, with the same ease and certainty with which one can summon the servant to one's hotel bedroom. An attendant now sleeps hard by the instrument at South Foreland and if at any moment he is awakened by the electric bell rung from the lightship he is able to ring up in turn the Ramsgate lifeboat and, if need be, direct it to the spot where its services are required within a few minutes of the call for help.

Ironically, it was the East Goodwin lightvessel herself that transmitted the first radio distress signal on 3 March 1899, when she was run down by a steamship. Lifeboats were despatched from Dover without delay.

Trinity House acquired the North and South Foreland lighthouses in 1832, shortly before the Act of 1836, the Admiralty transferring them direct. By this time the establishment of the South Goodwin lightvessel had rendered the leading capability of the South Foreland lights redundant and the front tower was abandoned. This old lighthouse remains, neglected and dull by comparison with its shining white and battlemented brother. The old front tower teeters on the edge of the receding cliff, an interesting relic of a former age. In 1872, largely on the advice of Michael Faraday, then scientific adviser to the Corporation, Trinity House introduced electric power to the Forelands which became the first light-houses in the world to use electricity. Today North Foreland is an important station and has radio data and control links with a number of automatic offshore aids to navigation.

The Goodwins remain a danger to shipping and various attempts have been made to erect a seamark on the sands themselves. None has been successful. On 10 September 1840 a Captain Bullock erected a safety beacon, or refuge, which doubled as a navigational mark, but it was washed away shortly afterwards. Spurred on by this example, Trinity House attempted to site unlit beacons on the sands by sinking hulks rigged with masts and topmarks, ballasting and forcing them to the bottom by loading them with boulders. Although the hulks appeared at first to hold firmly, they vanished after the first gales. Attempts to find bedrock by driving iron screws down through the sand also met with no success. But these efforts made in the 1840s and 1850s reflect the greatly changed attitude of Trinity House after 1836. Gone are the prevarications and objections. From a role of overseer and the enforced owner of a few lighthouses, Trinity House had moved on to embrace the confidence and innovative enterprise of the Victorian era.

CHAPTER FIVE

THE GREAT HIGHWAY

The Needles.

It is at the narrow bottleneck of the Strait of Dover that one becomes acutely aware of the sea as a highway of international trade. The stream of ships of every size and type is endless, outward bound for the four corners of the earth, or inward for the great ports of Europe. Between the South Foreland and Dungeness the Strait opens out to become the English Channel.

Above this busy scene, set in the old bastions of Langdon Battery, to the east of Dover, the radar station of HM Coastguard watches over maritime safety and the movements of all ships in the Dover Strait. Ready to co-ordinate the several arms of the rescue services and linked to the French radar station at Cap Gris Nez, it is ready to cope with any possible disaster such as a collision, perhaps involving an oil tanker and threatening massive pollution to the coasts of Britain and France. Today the two nations are eager to co-operate but evidence of former hostility exists in the fortifications of Henry VIII, whose three castles at Sandown, Deal and Walmer begin a long chain of defence along the south coast and augment the more ancient castle at Dover itself. Dover has been fortified continuously since the Iron Age, and the remains of the Roman pharos are still to be found within the castle ramparts. Built immediately after the annexation of the island of Britain by the Emperor Claudius in AD 43, the tower marked a landing place for the Roman supply ships sent from Gaul. Julius Caesar's "reconnaissance in force", a century earlier, had landed on the inhospitable beach at Deal, a few miles up the coast, but a small river dividing the cliffs at Dover provided a rudimentary harbour for the invading armies of Claudius. The main castle was constructed by Henry II in the twelfth century and played its part in the key dramas of English history: in the long struggle between the baronage and the Crown, in the English Civil War, and right up until our own times. During the Napoleonic War a series of ingenious tunnels and outer defences, well-lined with guns, was built under the direction of Sir John Burgoyne, the play-writing general who had surrendered a British army to the American rebels at Saratoga in 1777. A more sober officer than "Gentleman Johnny" and an almost neglected hero, Sir John Moore, trained the immortal Light Division upon the glacis of Dover Castle. After Moore's death at Corunna in 1809, the Light Division went on to become Wellington's brightest sword in the long slog of the Peninsular War.

Dover Harbour is an artificial harbour constructed at the turn of the century and today the highly sophisticated ferries of Britain, France and Belgium ply their trade from Dover with bewildering speed, making it the busiest port in the kingdom. Not only vast numbers of tourists but huge fleets of heavy lorries daily haul the merchandise of the EEC on and off the ferries, on to the motorways, autobahns and *routes-nationales* of the member nations.

West of Dover, the cliffs continue, great shorn buttresses of cretaceous chalk from which Shakespeare made Edgar look down and cry aloud for dizziness, that his blind father, King Lear, should know where they were. Alas, the "choughs

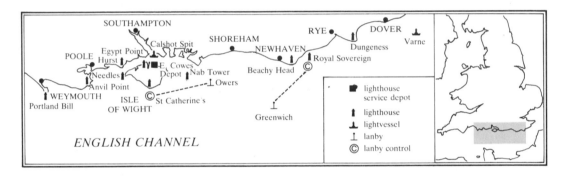

that wing the midway air" are no longer there and the cliffs begin to diminish at Folkestone. Here the high land swings north, while the coast drops down to that vulnerable level that set our forefathers a-jitter at the prospect of Napoleonic invasion. Here more Martello towers are to be found, flanking the old Roman settlement at Dymchurch and the sluices that control the draining of Romney Marsh. So vulnerable did the government consider the area that during the French invasion scare of 1800 to 1805 they had the Royal Military Canal dug, convinced that although a landing on the marsh could not be prevented, at least the canal would be defensible. Happily it was never put to the test, for it is extremely unlikely that the odd assortment of sea-fencibles, yeomanry and militia could have stood against Napoleon's veterans. The area remained wild and lawless, a haunt of smugglers despite (or perhaps because of) the two ancient towns that stand upon it. One of the original Cinque Ports, the town of Romney was situated on the River Rother. During a great storm in 1287 the river became so swollen that it abruptly changed its course and ran into the sea on the opposite side of Dungeness through Rye, destroying in the process some fifty taverns and twelve churches. The second ancient town upon Romney Marsh is Lydd whose former importance is indicated by the size and magnificence of its church where

Thomas Wolsey was once rector. Unfortunately the tall steeple has been responsible for several maritime disasters. Distinct against the sky, it had "the forme of the saile of some talle ship" so that many mariners laid their course towards it. A vessel approaching up-Channel from the west, seeking to round the headland of Dungeness, would not see the low coast of yellow shingle that lay in her track until it was too late. With a following wind and a flood tide, she would become "embayed" and unable to weather the point. Even today the shoreline is difficult to see, so that the huge monolithic power stations and the lighthouses on Dungeness seem to float mysteriously above the sea, anchored to the higher ground inland by an umbilical cord of pylons and wires.

Dungeness is the greatest shingle foreland on the English coast, constantly shifting under the remorseless influence of the tides. Whereas on the east coast of England this movement is southwards, on the south coast it is towards the east. The eastern flank of Dungeness is growing as the western vanishes, a circumstance one hopes the designers of the nuclear power stations took into account! Their perception of the remoteness of the headland is shared by that most misnamed British bird, the common gull, whose only breeding place in England is on Dungeness.

Off the ness, the tides run strongly and it was claimed that over a thousand seamen were lost annually "for want of a light". This lack of a lighthouse was laid before the Privy Council of King James I who referred the matter to Trinity House. The Corporation declined to assume responsibility but raised no objection to a courtier, Edward Howard, providing a light. Accordingly, in August 1615, King James granted a patent to Howard, empowering him to levy one penny per ton from all ships passing the ness during the succeeding forty years. Howard immediately built a brick tower which showed a coal fire. It seems, however, that once they had their light, the merchants who had called for it had no intention of paying any dues. Certainly Howard found the money impossible to collect and soon made over his interest to the appropriately named William Lamplough, Clerk of the Royal Kitchen. For all the incongruity of his title, Lamplough made a better manager than his predecessor and shrewdly appointed royal customs officials to act as his sub-agents in all ports. This was effective enough to cause the merchants to wail and, later in the century, to provide Pepys with evidence for condemning the profits on private lighthouses as "a burden upon trade". Trinity House added another objection. In 1621 a petition was presented to Parliament for the suppression of the light as "a nuisance to navigation". This extraordinary claim seems to stem from the poor quality of the light, probably due to the substitution of candles for coal made because of difficulties in transporting coal to such a remote spot. The result was a directive sent from Parliament to Lamplough to improve the quality of the light. The citizens of Rye were also jealous of Lamplough's profits. Their harbour was silting, their wealth diminishing and they too petitioned Parliament, arguing that the idea for the lighthouse had originated from their own corporation and that they were entitled to its ownership. But Lamplough's position was unassailable and, to be fair, he did build a new tower, closer to the sea, with a better light. Upon its illumination in 1635, the first tower was knocked down.

Lamplough disappears from history during the turmoil of the English Civil War and, during the Commonwealth, ownership of the light is obscure. There appears to have been a threat of demolition by the landlord, the Earl of Thanet, for non-payment of ground rent, but the Lord Protector, Oliver Cromwell, with his customary good sense, put a stop to that, considering it was not fitting that

*A lighthouse has stood on Dungeness since 1615. The present
tower was built in 1961 and its light is visible over twenty-seven miles.*

"the safety of many lives and the State's [i.e. naval] ships should be left to the will of the Earl of Thanet". Whoever Lamplough's successor was (we do not know his name), he retained ownership until after the Restoration of Charles II for in 1668 Trinity House took the unusual step of summoning him before its own court to admonish him for failure to keep good lights. By 1746 the recession of the sea had rendered the lighthouse increasingly useless. Nothing seems to have been done about this, however, until Samuel Wyatt designed a new lighthouse which was erected in 1792. Argand lamps run on sperm oil were fitted to the 120-foot tower. It was inspected by the famous Scottish lighthouse engineer, Robert Stevenson, in 1818 and he (as usual) found something to complain about and reported that he found "the tower had been in danger of falling and was secured by four buttresses". The tower had, in fact, been struck by lightning, a common hazard for all lighthouses. But despite Stevenson's remarks, Wyatt's tower lasted until 1904. At the time of Stevenson's visit, because of "the superannuated state of the lightkeeper", the light was attended by a Mr Cobb, the agent for the owner who at this period was Mr Coke, the agricultural experimentalist, of Holkham Hall in Norfolk, who derived £7,500 from the light dues in 1823 alone.

Following the 1836 Act of Parliament, Trinity House acquired the lighthouse and in 1862 electric light was installed. The "incompetence" of the keepers, as we have seen, resulted in a return to oil to supply the huge lamp of 850 candlepower, surrounded by glass prisms which increased the illuminating power by a hundredfold. At this time, the exterior of the tower was painted in black and white horizontal bands to make it more conspicuous during daylight. In the late nineteenth century keepers' dwellings were built round the base and these have survived the 1904 demolition. Then, once again, the recession of the shore forced the building of another tower, erected in brick by Messrs Patrick and Co. of London. This was 136 feet high, 38 feet in base diameter and also painted black and white. In 1960 it was obscured by the building of the first nuclear power station and the Central Electricity Generating Board paid for a replacement, sited 485 yards eastward and in service by November 1961. This tower was built from pre-cast concrete rings, five feet high, six inches thick and twelve feet in diameter. The characteristic black and white colouring was impregnated at the casting stage and is thus permanent. Today the light is powered by a sealed beam unit using 200-watt reflector lamps, projecting a single flash every ten seconds, visible over twenty-seven miles and measured at just under two million candelas.

It was off this bight between the South Foreland and Dungeness, close to the Varne Shoal, that there occurred the most modern of those disasters that seem needed to provoke improvements to safety at sea. On the morning of Monday, 11 January 1971, the Peruvian cargo ship *Paracas* collided with the tanker *Texaco Caribbean*. *Paracas* limped to safety but the tanker was cut in two and both parts sank, immediately forming a serious danger to navigation. The Dover Strait is divided longitudinally into traffic "lanes", one for ships bound down-channel, one for ships bound up-channel, with two coastal zones, one French, one English, which are deemed omni-directional and for coastal traffic only. Through traffic is bound to use either the west- or the east-bound lane. The west-bound lane is already severely restricted by the Varne Shoal and the *Texaco Caribbean* sank in the middle of it.

The Trinity House vessel *Siren* was immediately despatched from Harwich to locate, mark and survey the wreck, preparatory to buoying it. Despite her presence, early the following morning, the West German cargo ship *Brandenburg* sliced herself open on one section of the tanker and sank like a stone with considerable loss of life. In the days that followed, the three wrecks were located, buoyed and marked by two lightvessels. But ships continued to pass perilously close to the wrecks, ignoring the warnings issued by the lightvessels and the broadcasts of the coast radio stations. On the evening of 27 February the Greek vessel *Niki* entered the buoyed cordon, struck the wreckage and sank. Ten bodies, including that of a woman, were recovered. At the subsequent inquiries it emerged that confusion existed over the marking of wrecks. This varied from country to country and the lighthouse authorities agreed to combine to produce a new internationally-agreed buoyage system. Earlier attempts to do this had been disrupted by political arguments and two World Wars. But now, following these tragic losses, the world's many buoyage systems have been reduced to two: the IALA (International Association of Lighthouse Authorities) System A which was adopted in Europe, Asia and Africa, and IALA System B, adopted in North and South America.

The Dover Strait ends at Dungeness and opens out into the English Channel. To the west of Dungeness lies Rye Harbour on the estuary of the River Rother. A few miles or so up river, the ancient town of Rye was once granted equal status with the Cinque Ports and supplied successive English kings with ships to enable them to pursue their dynastic quarrels with the French monarchy. In 1377 the French attacked the town and almost completely destroyed it and it was walled as a consequence. However nothing could stop the gradual silting of the Rother, and Rye declined gracefully to become one of the most charming of English sea-towns. It still possesses a fishing fleet, operating on the inshore fishing grounds, but the ship-building yards which once produced fine coasting schooners and ketches are gone. Trinity House had its last sailing lighthouse tender, the *Mermaid*, built at Rye as late as 1865.

To the east of Rye the high land reappears on the coast at Fairlight Down. For generations Fairlight was a conspicuous navigation mark (it is mentioned in *Spanish Ladies*) but has never sported a lighthouse because extensive shoals lie offshore and vessels rarely close the coast west of Fairlight. Massive erosion has taken place. There is supposed to have been a natural harbour at Hastings at the time of the Norman invasion in 1066 and the remains of old rocks lie now beneath the sea, forming the Royal Sovereign Shoal off Eastbourne. Buoyed since 1850, a lightvessel was added twenty-five years later. In 1971 a prefabricated light-tower was completed, built of concrete in two sections on the beach at Newhaven. In 1970 the base and telescopic tower were towed out and sunk in position. The following summer the accommodation block which incorporated a helicopter landing-pad, the lantern and ancillary equipment, was floated out and dropped over the extending tower as the tide fell away. The pontoons on which it had been brought were cut away and during the succeeding weeks the telescopic tower was gradually jacked up to its present height. In addition to providing the usual services, the Royal Sovereign monitors the performance of a number of remote-controlled buoys. The optic comprises three ground and polished Fresnel lenses of 375-mm focal length, revolving at one turn a minute around a 1000-watt, 100-volt lamp, thus showing a group of three flashes every twenty seconds with an intensity of two and a half million candelas. This powerful light is driven by a special gearless motor with only one moving part.

The Needles. The three 100-foot pinnacles of chalk are the remnants of a ridge that once joined the Isle of Wight to the mainland. The lighthouse on the tip was built in 1859 and is one of the few stations that still has to be relieved by boat rather than helicopter.

*The 142-foot lighthouse at Beachy Head is dwarfed by the
sheer cliff drop at the end of the South Downs.*

Off Hastings, what may be the remains of William the Conqueror's harbour, the Bo-Peep Rocks, extend out to sea. The well-known nursery rhyme is said to have been composed for the daughter of a local Bulverhythe publican during the eighteenth century when smuggling was at its height. It is full of allusion, particularly the assertion that the "lost sheep" will find their own way home. The tails of the sheep were the casks of contraband brandy and the silly sheep the wily smugglers themselves who doubtless cloaked their activities under a yokel-like stupidity in the presence of the Revenue Officers when the song was sung for the little girl's amusement.

All along the south coast we can see fortifications that bear witness to the recurrent spectre of invasion. Henry VIII's forts extend to the West Country; Lord Palmerston's so-called "follies" even further; but the long line of Martello towers ends where the chalk cliffs of Beachy Head and the Seven Sisters drop abruptly to the sea. The reappearance of this chalk, more readily eroded than the bedrock beneath the Royal Sovereign, takes deep water almost up to the foot of the cliffs. Ten miles west of the Sovereign stands the red and white banded tower of Beachy Head lighthouse at the foot of the cliffs and about two hundred yards to seaward of them. It is thought that a light was shown from the cliff-top as early as 1690, but this is inconclusive and certainly no continuous light was shown until 1828 when Trinity House ordered James Walker, their principal lighthouse engineer, to construct a low stone tower (which still exists) on the cliff. So high was this, though, that the light was usually obscured by orographic cloud. This failure to take into account the formation of low cloud upon cliff-tops occurs frequently elsewhere. However, it was erosion of the cliffs that was given as the reason for building the present lighthouse in 1900.

A foundation of hard chalk was found 550 feet from the cliff and, as this only uncovered at low water, a caisson was built in which the footings of the tower were excavated by hand as it was feared that explosives would split the bedrock. A heavy iron sheerlegs was fitted to the rim of the caisson to receive the seaward end of an aerial runway from the cliff-top high above. The main wire for this was six inches in diameter with a breaking strain of 120 tons and down this runway 3,600 tons of dressed Cornish granite were slung. The work took two years. Today the light is visible except in conditions of dense fog, twice every twenty seconds, whether or not there is cloud on the cliffs above. The station is now automatic, electric power being supplied to a transformer set in the chalk above and conveyed to the lighthouse by thin wires slung across the gap.

It was off Beachy Head that the Royal Navy suffered its worst defeat at the hands of the French. Depleted by King William III's expedition to Ireland in 1690, the Anglo-Dutch Channel fleet under the Earl of Torrington was attacked by a superior French fleet of seventy-seven line of battleships under the Comte de Tourville. Falling back eastwards, Torrington, who commanded some fifty-six ships was eventually compelled to offer battle off Beachy Head. Faulty dispositions of the vessels resulted in the Dutch under Evertsen bearing the brunt of the attack by the French. Fortunately the wind dropped and the allies were able to withdraw. Torrington destroyed his damaged ships to prevent them falling into French hands while Tourville failed to pursue and contented himself with retiring down Channel and burning Teignmouth. Torrington was relieved of his command, although he continued to be an Elder Brother of Trinity House.

The tremendous chalk cliffs run westwards towards Brighton, dipping in regular formation to expose old river valleys which indicate the encroachment of the sea to a remarkable degree. The gradually descending valleys have been cut off many feet above sea-level, to leave the gentle undulations of the Seven Sisters. Of the residue of this erosion there is scarcely a trace, for deep water closes the shore. Two rivers remain, the Cuckmere and the Ouse, which now emerges at Newhaven, although formerly it reached the sea at Seaford, two miles eastward. In 1579 a ferocious gale destroyed the river mouth and the "New Haven" was formed. In 1847 the cross-Channel packet service was inaugurated by paddle-steamers. Since the 1860s the entrance has been guarded by Fort Newhaven, one of Palmerston's forts built to counter the resurgent maritime power of France under Napoleon III.

West of Newhaven the coast is dominated by the distant heights of the South Downs, crowned by the ancient and conspicuous wooded summit of Chanctonbury Ring. Along the shoreline successive generations have changed the fishing village of Brighthelmstone into the holiday town of Brighton. Today the pollution of its beaches is more likely to induce than cure the glandular diseases a certain Dr Russel claimed it eliminated when he first recommended sea-bathing in 1750. Its seamier side is well illustrated by Graham Greene in his novel about petty criminals, *Brighton Rock*.

Unlike the Ouse, the eastward swing of the River Adur has not been destroyed by the sea and has been adapted to form the docks at Shoreham. The huge power station chimneys alongside are visible many miles to sea but now invisible from seaward is the disused lighthouse built in 1846. Shoreham is protected by another of Palmerston's sea defences and, in spite of being used by medium-sized ships, is fronted by increasingly shallow water. The build-up of offshore dangers increases until, off the low promontory of Selsea Bill, a vast area of rocks and shoals extends up to seven miles to the south. Several buoys mark these reefs and a narrow passage through can be found, but on the whole ships avoid them. As long ago as 1788, the Admiralty persuaded Trinity House to establish a lightvessel on the Owers station, to the southward of the area. Because of the poor holding ground for the vessel's anchors the lightship frequently dragged off her station and once got as far as St Valéry-en-Caux in France. In 1973 the lightvessel was replaced by a large, automatic buoy giving a light comparable to the former lightvessel.

The coast between the Owers and Anvil Point is the focus of maritime Britain. It contains the great naval port of Portsmouth, the mercantile port of Southampton and the yachting centre of Cowes. The waters of the Solent and

Spithead are sheltered by the Isle of Wight and provide ample room for even the less well-heeled to mess about in boats. Once, the geologists claim, the River Frome flowed eastwards from what is now Poole Harbour, north of a chalk ridge that extended from Purbeck to Bembridge and included the Isle of Wight. Into the Frome during this period flowed the Avon and (another) Stour, which now emerges through Christchurch, the Test and the Itchen (which now fill South-

Painting the buoys on deck is a regular part of the maintenance work done by the Trinity House vessels.

ampton Water), the Hamble, Beaulieu and Lymington Rivers, together with several lesser streams, all combining to fill the great valley that is now the Solent. The sinking of land and the erosion of the chalk between Old Harry Rocks off Swanage and the Needles, enabled the tide to break through into the valley. Now the tide flows round the Isle of Wight, from both directions, meeting in South-ampton Water and resulting in a long period of high water and a double high tide at Southampton.

The great docks of Southampton have been badly hit by the recession and industrial problems. Once the port from which the great Atlantic liners departed for the United States, Southampton has lost most of its massively invested container traffic to Felixstowe, although the oil refinery at Fawley still handles tankers of enormous size. Portsmouth continues to prosper, largely unaffected by the ebb and flow of commercial considerations. Portchester Castle on its northern shore was once another Roman fortress under the jurisdiction of the

Servicing a buoy at night.

Count of the Saxon shore and was largely rebuilt during the Middle Ages. It was from Portchester that Henry V sailed on his vainglorious and nearly disastrous Agincourt campaign in 1415 and nearly four hundred years later 4,000 unfortunate French prisoners were incarcerated within its walls during the Napoleonic Wars. Portsmouth itself was fortified by Henry VIII, who built Southsea Castle there. When the French invaded the Isle of Wight in 1545, just after the castle's completion, it was to Southsea that the king repaired to watch his fabulously expensive new fleet go into action. Although the French withdrew, King Henry witnessed the mysterious sinking of the *Mary Rose* in Spithead. The defences were improved by Palmerston in about 1850 because Napoleon III, who came to power after the French monarchy fell in 1848, alarmed the British government by dramatically increasing the power of the French fleet. As well as reinforcing Southsea Castle and improving the defences of the entrance to Portsmouth Harbour, Palmerston built six huge fortresses on the heights of Portsdown Hill, commanding the dockyard below. Offshore he built four more forts, one protecting the anchorage at St Helen's (on the east coast of the Isle of Wight) and three in the approaches to Spithead.

Portsmouth is dominated by the Royal Naval Dockyard and the ships of the fleet and they in turn are dominated by the Royal Navy's shrine, HMS *Victory*,

Nelson's flagship at Trafalgar. Built fifty years before Trafalgar, *Victory* was a first-rate line-of-battleship, the flagship of successive commanders-in-chief, including some of Britain's most distinguished seamen. Near her lie the remains of the *Mary Rose*. One of the first ships to form part of the "standing navy" of Henry VIII, she was one of the first warships to mount and fire a broadside. This introduction of massed artillery along the sides of a ship was to form the pattern of naval warfare for three hundred years, fleets manoeuvring in "line-of-battle" to concentrate their firepower. It was admirals like Rodney, Duncan and Nelson who saw the weaknesses in this dogma and exploited it through superior seamanship, so it is fitting that the *Mary Rose* lies near *Victory*. Nevertheless Henry's first action with his fleet of broadside-firing ships was not impressive. They failed to employ their advantage and the French, who were attacking the English fleet off the very beaches of Portsmouth itself, were only driven off with difficulty. In the chaos of the action the *Mary Rose* unaccountably sank. Various theories have been put forward which vary from a mutiny, an incapacity among the crew due to dysentery, to an ingress of water through the low gun-ports. The precise cause will never be known, even though the sinking took place in front of the astonished king and his suite who had ridden out to see the French given their trouncing. The fleets met again the same year (1545) and on this occasion the broadside was used for the first time, but by then the *Mary Rose* was lying in the ooze.

Near the place from which the *Mary Rose* was raised, lie the bones of the navy's most guarded scandal. Towards the end of the American War of Independence, the Channel Fleet was anchored in Spithead and Admiral Kempenfelt was on board his flagship, HMS *Royal George*. The *Royal George* had been Hawke's flagship at the running victory of Quiberon Bay in 1759 and was known as a swift sailer with a tall rig. On 29 August 1782 she was listed for some superficial repairs to a sea-cock just below her waterline. Aboard her were some 800 men together with their wives, children and the usual collection of usurers, vendors and whores then permitted on board ships of war at anchor in home waters. Suddenly the huge ship trembled and lay over on her beam ends. In a remarkably short space of time, she filled with water and sank beneath the murky waters of Spithead. The inquiry gave out that a gust of wind had laid her over excessively and that the water had rushed in through the lower deck gun-ports. (A reason, ironically enough, which was also advanced for the loss of the *Mary Rose*.) In secret the inquiry determined that the timbers of the *Royal George* were so rotten that they had been stove inwards by the unusual water pressure caused by her listing. William Cowper's magnificent poem, *Toll for the Brave*, quite unconsciously gave the authorities a much needed let-out. Cowper attributed the disaster to the sudden lurch "as the land breeze shook the shrouds" and the government did little to disabuse the public of this notion, although the truth was known throughout the British fleet. Behind the disaster lay the appalling corruption in the Royal Dockyards, the failure to dry-dock the ships properly and the totally false assumption that timbers exposed to the weather when the ship was built necessarily acquired longevity. There were even cases of warships being constructed of timber that was already rotten, several being condemned before they were complete.

There is one more wreck near Portsmouth which is of some interest. One of the few French ships to escape destruction or capture at Trafalgar was the French 74-gun battleship, *Duguay Trouin*. Built at Rochefort in 1800 and named after a Breton corsair, she was brought to battle a few days after Trafalgar by the ships of Sir Richard Strachan, off Cape Ortegal, as she tried to get back to a French port. Her captain, Touffet, defended his ship with great gallantry but was killed in the action. *Duguay Trouin* had all her masts shot down and numbers of her crew killed or wounded before she surrendered. She was then brought to Plymouth under jury-rig and taken into the Royal Navy as HMS *Implacable*. Under this name she saw service in the Baltic, but by 1855 had been relegated to a Boys' Training Ship. Used in both wars, she was paid off in 1947. Attempts to preserve her failed and on 2 December 1949, the anniversary of Napoleon's coronation, flying the ensigns of France and Great Britain and in the presence of ships of both nations, she was scuttled, nine miles south of the Owers lightvessel.

Between the remains of the *Royal George* in Spithead and the *Implacable* off the Owers, the eastern entrance to the Solent is marked by the Nab Tower. During the First World War, this curious structure with its slight list was being towed to the Dover Strait to form part of an anti-submarine boom across the narrow waterway there. Unfortunately, the concrete tower sunk on passage, slap-bang in the fairway, and a light was promptly put upon it. For many years it was jointly manned by the Royal Navy as a signal station and by Trinity House as a lighthouse, but both organizations have now evacuated it. Today Nab Tower remains an automatic lighthouse, marking the busy main approach to Southampton and Portsmouth.

The western entrance is more hazardous and narrower. The Solent forces its way between the Isle of Wight and Hampshire past Hurst Point, dominated by the mass of Hurst Castle, another of Henry VIII's defensive works. This was briefly a prison for Charles I on his journey from Carisbrooke Castle to his trial at Westminster in the winter of 1648. It was reinforced by Palmerston at the same time as Forts Albert and Victoria were constructed on the Isle of Wight side of the narrows. The remains of the old chalk ridge across this entrance to the Solent combines with cross tides to make the Needles Channel difficult for large ships. The navigable gap known as the Bridge is narrow and marked by buoys. To assist vessels making the transit, Trinity House maintains a high and low lighthouse within Hurst Castle to lead the mariner in through the gap in the time-honoured method. Towards the end of the eighteenth century, Trinity House was approached to establish lights at the Needles and St Catherine's Point, the southern extremity of the Isle of Wight. About 1786 Trinity House completed work on three lights, all to the designs of a Mr Jupp, a surveyor to the East India Company. A light was exhibited from Hurst Castle, another at St Catherine's and the third on the cliffs high above the Needles where, predictably, it was obscured by mist and low cloud. In 1812 a second, higher tower was built at Hurst, so that a transit of the two lights within the castle led the mariner through the Bridge. The poor siting of the lights at the Needles and St Catherine's will, by now, come as no surprise. The former was 474 feet above sea level; the latter 750. Despite their situation, they remained in use until James Walker designed and oversaw (at a cost of £20,000) a new tower built of granite at the very extremity of the Needles

The Nab Tower was intended to be part of an anti-submarine boom across the Dover Strait during the First World War. But it sank under tow and has been used as a lighthouse ever since.

themselves. The tower was untapered but the base was stepped, to break up the action of the sea. The granite was banded in red and white and the occulting light was exhibited in sectors: red over the Shingles and Dolphin Banks; green over the Warden Bank and white through the narrows past Hurst Castle and to seaward. It is an impossible station on which to construct a helipad and remains manned by three keepers who are relieved every month by boat.

St Catherine's bore a light as early as 1323. A certain Walter de Godyton built a chapel in which he paid a priest to say masses for the souls of his family and to show a light by night for the benefit of shipping. This practice lasted until the Reformation when the endowment was abolished. The early tower was replaced in 1840 by an octagonal structure in ashlar stone which rose in diminishing tiers. When this also proved too tall, it was reduced in height by removing sections from the two tiers, dropping the lantern over forty feet. By 1932, when the fog signal house became undermined, it was replaced by a smaller replica of the lantern tower, giving rise to the local name of "Cow and Calf". The lighthouse was attacked by the Luftwaffe during the Second World War and incendiary bombs set fire to the lighthouse and dwellings. The keepers were burned to death and their bodies had to be dug out of the wreckage. Today, St Catherine's flashes every five seconds, the beam of its powerful five and a quarter million candela light visible for thirty miles on a clear, dark night. A red sector light shines over the Atherfield Ledge along the coast to the north-west; a radio beacon and a Super Tyfon fog signal are also fitted. From this lighthouse a telemetric link monitors and controls the Owers buoy, twenty-four miles to the east.

Across the double bight of Christchurch and Poole Bays, lies the chalk headland of Anvil Point. On the shore of these bays are the towns of Milford-on-Sea, Christchurch and Bournemouth, situated on low cliffs or behind shingle beaches. Bournemouth Bay is cut in soft Tertiary deposits and fossils can be found in the undercliff at Barton-on-Sea. Hengistbury Head has been fortified since earliest times and behind it is Christchurch, originally called Twynham, a Saxon allusion to its lying between the Stour and Avon. Poole Harbour is shallow and largely composed of mudflats. Into it drain the much diminished Frome and the delightfully named Piddle, which modern cartographers regrettably call the Trent. As there are as many Trents as Ouses, Stours and Avons, the name Piddle seems preferable. Poole has a small commercial quay and Brownsea Island, set just inside the entrance, boasts a Henrician fort.

At Swanage chalk stacks known as Old Harry and Old Harry's Wife provide evidence of a prehistoric connection with the distant Needles. The cliffs of Studland Bay swing west at Durlston Head and the chalk retreats inland, being fronted along the coast by jurassic limestone. This shows the dramatic results of erosion and folding. At Lulworth the sea has broken through to form an almost totally enclosed pool, while a similar process is in the course of maturation at Stair Hole. Neither of these features is visible from the sea, although the disappearance of the limestone and reappearance of the chalk can be clearly seen at Worbarrow Bay. Durdle Door, a limestone arch, and Bat's Head Hole are two other remarkable features along this coast which is not often closed by ships of any size. Most ships make an offing west of the Needles, to avoid the tidal race that boils over the rock ledges to the south of St Alban's Head, or the worse one off Portland Bill. As the outward-bound mariner takes a final bearing of Anvil Point lighthouse, built in 1881 upon the cliff top above St Alban's Race, he will be aware of the rising massif of Portland itself. Geologically an island, it is linked to the mainland by the long shingle spit of Chesil Beach. Portland's artificial harbour was built in the 1840s by convicts awaiting transportation to Australia. They were accommodated in the Verne, a prison on the island's summit, damp

*The lighthouse an Anvil Point in Dorset stands at the end
of a coastal path through Durlston Country Park.
Colonies of sea-birds inhabit the chalk cliffs.*

Top: Gathering rain clouds cast their shadows on the choppy seas. Above: The great naval port of Portsmouth where Henry VIII watched the sinking of the Mary Rose *still flourishes today.*

At the beginning of the eighteenth century three lighthouses were built at the Casquets in the Channel Islands to distinguish them from the lights at the Lizard and in the Scilly Isles. Today one tower houses the fog signal and another acts as a store and support for the helipad.

A cable ship off Plymouth.

*Below: HM Yacht Britannia is among the vessels
anchored in St Peter Port, Guernsey. Bottom: The
Eddystone lighthouse stands fourteen miles to the south
of Plymouth, warning ships of the "twenty-three rust red
granite rocks" of the notorious Eddystone Reef.*

and cloud-shrouded, a wretched place from which to take their departure for the Antipodes.

The great toe of Portland Bill extends far out into the Channel tide, its obstruction accelerating the speed of the tidal stream. Forced seawards by the long expanse of Chesil Beach, the flood from Lyme Bay whirls round the Bill in a gigantic circular race. This dies at slack water, only to revive as the ebb runs in the opposite direction. At half-tide, the period at which ebb and flood run strongest, a great whorl of water circulates off the point and, when acted upon by a strong wind, this produces high, unstable, breaking seas. These tide-races become an increasingly common feature of the coast to the west of the Isle of Wight, as we leave the softer and younger bedrocks of the south-east. The hard headlands of the west are more resistant to erosion and their interruption to the coastal flow of the tides provokes the phenomenon. The height and instability of the waves caused in these races can come as a considerable surprise to the inexperienced sailor. The forces acting on the waves make them topple so that they can break on board ships and do considerable damage. This danger is compounded by the difficulty of steering a course. Along the length of a vessel the tide may exert a vicious turning movement, against which the rudder is impotent. In the days of sail these hazards were well understood. Portland Bill was a place to be avoided and it is not surprising to find that our old friend Sir John Clayton selected the Bill as a site for a lighthouse. Nothing came of his scheme but the merchants of Weymouth revived the idea some years later. Their petition to George I was opposed by Trinity House on the dubious grounds of expense, but the Corporation obviously then had second thoughts, for in 1716 Trinity House gave a lease to a number of local worthies, named as William Borrett, Francis Browne and others who were anxious to build a lighthouse. The patent clearly describes the notorious dangers of navigating the Bill: "The passage by the island of Portland in dark nights being very dangerous and many ships . . . in a little space of time lost there."

Two lighthouses were built by Borrett and his colleagues, employing a builder called Charles Langridge to carry out the work. Coal fires were kindled in glazed lanterns on 29 September 1716 but they proved badly kept. In 1752, observing the lighthouses from their yacht, two of the Elder Brethren reported that "it was nigh two hours after sunset before any light appeared in either of the lighthouses". At the expiry of the lease in 1767, Trinity House took over the management of the lights and rebuilt them at a cost of £2,000, fitting the then brand new argand lights with reflectors and, in the case of the front light, additional lenses. This light was reckoned to be of 1,500 candlepower which was quite powerful for the period. The changing attitude of Trinity House is reflected in the inscription over the doorway which bore the legend that the lights were established "For the Direction and Comfort of Navigators; For the Benefit and Security of Commerce and for a lasting memorial of British Hospitality to All Nations this lighthouse was erected." Two 18-pound cannon were installed in

1798 to deter any French ships-of-war that might attempt to damage British trade by the destruction of the lighthouses, but there is no record of their being used.

New high and low lights were built in 1869, but at the turn of the century the idea of leading lights had very largely gone out of fashion. In 1906 the dwellings of the old lighthouses were converted to private use and a new tower was built on the extremity of the Bill, where the rock is fairly low and level, well below the cloud-base surrounding the prison. Until the present lighthouse was built on Dungeness, Portland was the tallest in the Service, a fine tapered white tower with a broad red band about its middle. The light-source is a 1,000-watt bulb which shines through a four-panel catadioptric lens-mounting which, revolving three times a minute, produces a group of four flashes every twenty seconds. The power of the light is rated at 3.37 million candelas. As well as having a fog signal, Portland Bill lighthouse is identified in fog by a racon marking the screen of any ship transmitting and receiving radar emissions in the vicinity.

Lying close, east of the Bill, there is a shoal known as the Shambles, marked by buoys and a red sector from the lighthouse on the Bill. The Shambles only compounds the dangers off Portland, but once clear of it the English Channel widens, the westbound mariner begins to sense the open Atlantic ahead of him. The Western Ocean swell pushes up the Channel to meet him and the pelagic birds appear again: gannets, skuas and shearwaters.

CHAPTER SIX

THE CHOPS OF
THE CHANNEL

Start Point.

On a map, the English Channel looks like a great mouth, open to the west. At its eastern end the nickname of the Goodwin Sands, the "Great Ship Swallower", seems doubly justified, while at the opposite, western end the open maw is equally aptly known as "the Chops of the Channel". To the west of Cherbourg, the lower jaw drops abruptly to the Breton coast, its mandible studded with the fangs of the Channel Islands and the Minquiers. Along the northern shore, the great incisors of Start Point and the Lizard stab southward, whilst the Eddystone, the Wolf and the Isles of Scilly lie in wait like the cast teeth of ancient dragons.

Lest my metaphors seem too purple, I must emphasize that this is how it would have seemed to generations of European seamen returning home, via the English Channel. It was often the most hazardous part of any distant voyage, particularly in the early days of Europe's maritime expansion. Its manifold dangers, encountered singly, might have been overcome, but together were often overwhelming. Fog and fierce tides combined to make periods of calm almost as feared as gales, while the onset of strong westerly winds could produce low visibility and heavy sea when opposing a Channel ebb. Furthermore a fair wind from the west could cast a square-rigged ship on a lee shore in one of the numerous bays if she was uncertain of her position. Even as late as the nineteenth century, much navigation was rudimentary. The main problem of establishing a ship's longitude was solved in the late eighteenth century by the invention of a reliable chronometer capable of withstanding an ocean voyage. Its value was proved by James Cook but this advance did not end navigational problems overnight. For a start, few ships carried chronometers for several years and even if they did, the Western Approaches are notorious for their overcast skies. Unless the navigator could observe a known heavenly body at the same time as the horizon, he was unable to calculate his position with any accuracy beyond the purely deductive process known as dead-reckoning.

Many hundreds of ships have been lost attempting to enter the English

Channel. In the autumn of 1707 a British fleet under Admiral Sir Clowdisley Shovell was returning from service in the Mediterranean. With a following gale and in thick weather the fleet, believing itself safe, set a course to take it up Channel. Alas, the squadron was well north of its reckoning and Shovell's flagship, HMS *Association*, ran too close to the Isles of Scilly, struck the Gilstone and was instantly dashed to pieces. Inshore of the *Association*, the *Eagle* and the

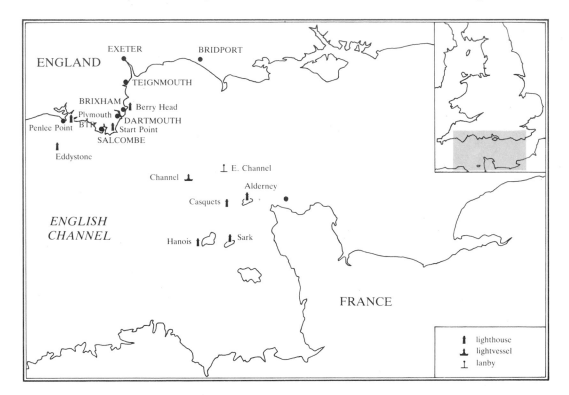

Romney shared the same fate. Several other ships were damaged and the fleet was thrown into the utmost confusion. One man out of the *Romney* was saved, but the remainder perished. Admiral Shovell himself was said to have been washed up, half-drowned, upon the beach at Porth Hellick, only to be murdered by an old woman for the jewelled rings he wore. "We were much to the northward of what was expected," reported the captain of the *Torbay* which narrowly escaped the fate of the flagship.

In 1744 Admiral Balchen on board HMS *Victory* entered the Channel, making for Spithead. The *Victory* struck the Casquets despite the presence of the lighthouses there and the admiral was lost with more than a thousand men. Balchen's death was probably due to the difficulty of handling these great ships. Enormous skill was needed to sail them and they required a great deal of room to manoeuvre. The lights were probably sighted but the ship would have struck before anything could be done to avoid the outlying spurs of the reef. Nelson's famous ship was built as the replacement for this ill-fated vessel.

In addition to the hazards of nature, there was also the malice of man. Although English law cast a stern eye upon anyone encouraging wrecks by exhibiting "false-lights", on the wild coasts of the west, in both Britain and France, a considerable amount of deliberate wrecking went on. Early proposals to build a lighthouse on the Lizard, for instance, were opposed locally by a population who relied on this gruesome means of subsistence during the winter months.

Not surprisingly, two of the earliest lighthouses were built at the western entrance to the Channel: St Agnes, in the Isles of Scilly and another on the French island of Ushant. So important were these considered that Great Britain and France signed a treaty to protect the light on Ushant from attack during hostilities. But these provisions did not stop catastrophic losses. The inability of mariners to have very much of an idea where they were in poor visibility made it important for them to recognize instantly any light that they were able to catch a glimpse of. Today it is possible to differentiate between one light and another by varying its characteristic, that is the period and number of its flashes. It may flash once every ten seconds, or a group flash of four every twenty seconds, as at Portland Bill. Before the introduction of the revolving apparatus, around the beginning of the nineteenth century, no such solution was available and the problem of distinguishing the three main landfall lights in the entrance of the Channel seemed insoluble. In 1690, when St Agnes was built in the Isles of Scilly, it was comparatively close to the Lizard. Since a mariner was so uncertain of his position, how could the Casquets lighthouse in the Channel Islands be identified? Despite the great distance separating them, it would not have been at all obvious to a mariner who might run into danger by mistaking one for another. There *was* a solution and it was pretty crude. When the Lizard was built the expedient was adopted of constructing two towers so that twin fires were shown, a contrast to the single one at St Agnes. In the case of the Casquets, three towers were built.

At the beginning of the eighteenth century, approaches were made to Thomas Le Cocq, owner of the dark cluster of rocks north-west of Alderney known as the Casquets. Le Cocq was introduced by an anonymous Elder Brother (with whom he later shared the profits of his lights) to Trinity House and on 3 June 1720 a patent was granted stipulating the erection of the three light-towers mentioned above. Named St Peter, St Paul and Dungeon, each supported an enclosed coal fire which the keeper and his family were supposed to maintain at an equal intensity. These were first lit on 30 October 1724. When Le Cocq's partner died, the secret agreement between them came to light and the dependants of the dead Elder Brother tried to retain the interest in the lighthouses. The matter went to law with the dependants claiming the Elder Brother had been "extraordinarily well skilled in the manner of placing, building and constructing lighthouses and had frequently superintended such works". Trinity House's reaction was distinctly unfraternal. They denied their quondam colleague had any technical abilities at all, stating that he was

> an entire stranger to the nature thereof and utterly unqualified to give Thomas Le Cocq any assistance therein ... he had never had the direction of, nor was concerned in, any building of that nature or kind, nor was ever in any lighthouse nor saw any lighthouse except in passing by the same at a distance at sea and that the lighthouses erected by Thomas Le Cocq were planned and designed and built and completed by the directions of William Norman who had before built several structures of like nature.

Le Cocq's income from the light at this time was not much and fluctuated during the frequent wars with France. In 1785 the lease expired and ownership reverted to Trinity House who promptly improved the optic by introducing argand lights and reflectors. Oddly enough, when revolving mountings were fitted in 1818, all three towers were retained and were still in use when the towers were raised in 1854. Shortly after this, however, new apparatus was installed in the western tower and the others were discontinued. Nevertheless, the towers remain in use, one as the housing for the fog signal, the third as a store and support for the helipad. The station was converted to electric power, generated on the rock, in 1952 and the modern characteristic is a group of five white flashes every thirty seconds of nearly 3 million candelas intensity. In common with the Channel Islands as a whole, during the Second World War the Casquets light was occupied by German troops who erected a number of defences. The remains of an anti-aircraft gun and a large compass-rose bearing German notation can still be seen in the compound, while the numerous shell-cases that may still be picked up indicate the station was frequently shot up by aircraft of the RAF. The garrison surrendered in 1944 to an armed party from the destroyer HMS *Lynx*, which included an Elder Brother and the local superintendent.

The Casquets is an outcrop of Armorican rock, the most north-westerly of the archipelago known as the Channel Islands. Jersey, Guernsey, Alderney, Herm and Sark are the principal inhabited islands and they are surrounded by numerous islets, rocks and reefs. Ten miles south of Jersey, the Plateau des Minquiers is a great submerged island and, like the others, the graveyard of many, many vessels of all types and periods.

Apart from the frequent violence of the weather on these exposed coasts, there is great tidal activity hereabouts, much more so than on the opposite side of the Channel. The tidal streams are more violent, the rise and fall greater than along the English shore. This is due to "coriolis", a spinning off to the right of the tide as it floods eastward into the Channel and a similar spinning off to the right as it ebbs to the westward. This is caused by the earth's rotation and its result is that the tidal range along the south coast of England is damped down, while that along the French coast, in particular around Brittany, west Normandy and the Channel

Islands, is greatly augmented since coriolis piles up the high-waters and empties out the lows. There are, therefore, areas of particular tidal violence which, when combined with contrary winds, can throw up a vicious, breaking sea such as in the race between Alderney and the Cotentin peninsula.

The whole area produces dramatic sea-scapes which seem idyllic under the blue of a summer sky. The rock formations can assume bizarre outlines, the home of thousands of breeding sea-birds in the spring. Plant-life produces a riot of colour and the islands attract many visitors. But under the leaden clouds of an

The lighthouse at Les Hanois, off south-west Jersey.

approaching depression, when the Atlantic loses its benign and blue good humour, it is a place to be avoided. The sight of the long swells building up to break in a welter of foam about the black fangs of Les Hanois, to suck and gurgle round the base of the lighthouse, expending vast amounts of kinetic energy in the remorseless attack of the sea upon the land is awe-inspiring. Behind the outpost of Les Hanois, the island of Guernsey lies like a right-angled triangle, its hypotenuse facing north-west, its base steep-to and lying east/west. The Atlantic has smashed itself against the hypotenuse, driving the habitable land eastwards, exposing the tougher cores of rocks and eating its inexorable way into the island, forming bays of sand between headlands of hard rock. As Guernsey slowly retreats before the onslaught, it leaves a mass of reefs to the westward, the most advanced at the south-west corner, Les Hanois. The Les Hanois lighthouse was built in 1862 and represented an important innovation in the construction of rock lighthouses. One of the problems that faced the early builders of these isolated towers was how to prevent the action of the sea from washing mortar out from between the blocks of masonry. The matter bedevilled early lighthouse engineers, particularly on the Eddystone, and until it was satisfactorily solved, their work has to be considered as experimental. The solution was devised by Nicholas Douglass, one of a family of lighthouse constructors who rarely get the credit they deserve.

The brilliant Scottish family of engineers, the Stevensons, have to some extent overshadowed their English counterparts, the Douglass family. Nicholas Douglass worked under James Walker (about whom we know little) around the middle of the nineteenth century. He seems to have been responsible for the construction of many of Walker's designs, but his name is never pre-eminent except in the case of Les Hanois. Both his sons rose to prominence in the profession, picking up a piecemeal education as they followed their father from one project to another. The elder, James, "was not only an engineer, but he was a blacksmith, a carpenter, and a mason in his own person, as well as a seaman". By the age of thirty-six James Douglass had become engineer-in-chief to Trinity House. Although a model of Victorian rectitude, he was not devoid of a certain flamboyance. We shall meet him again later. His brother, William, became chief civil engineer to the Commissioners for Irish Lights and his son was another civil engineer for Trinity House. Both William and James appear to have worked on Les Hanois.

Up until 1862 various methods had been used to join each stone to its neighbours to form one cohesive mass of granite. John Smeaton had used metal pins and marble dowels at the Eddystone; Robert Stevenson had dove-tailed adjacent blocks when building the Bell Rock in Scotland, but Nicholas Douglass further refined the method by dove-tailing vertically as well as laterally. This must have required enormous skill on the part of his masons and in actually fitting the stones on site, but it became the accepted method and ended the search for a cohesion in the structure that would enable it to resist the sea indefinitely. Since its construction Hanois lighthouse has been modernized in accordance with the improvements in lighting apparatus and other aids to navigation. The most recent alteration was the fitting in 1979 of a helicopter platform above the lantern. Les Hanois remains a manned "Rock Station" with two watches of three keepers, each of whom work a month on duty and a month ashore. They are flown out from Guernsey, like their colleagues at the Casquets, and no longer endure the often wet and uncomfortable boat trip that was formerly the only method of putting lighthouse keepers on to their lonely work-places.

Although Crown possessions, the Channel Islands are not part of the United

*A windy day on Start Point, south Devon. In 1891 five
ships were wrecked on the rocks below in one night.*

The light on the Bishop Rock, the most extreme south-westerly point of the reefs around the Scilly Isles.

Below: The low rocks and islets scattered around the Scilly Isles are deadly to ships and over the centuries have been responsible for countless wrecks.

Kingdom. Sark is ruled by a seigneur and is devoid of such modern contrivances as cars. The island is almost cut in two, the ithsmus at La Coupée connecting the smaller, south end to the main part. Mervyn Peake describes it as "wasp-waisted" in his whimsical novel *Mr Pye*. There are some spectacular bays and a tiny stone harbour at Le Creux on Sark's east side, that lies beneath beetling cliffs and is reached by a tunnel cut in the rock. Set into the cliffs above to avoid orographic cloud, stands Point Robert lighthouse. Its main function is to enable vessels to fix their positon when passing to the eastward of the Channel Islands and to avoid the pinnacle of the Blanchard Rock which lies several miles east of Point Robert.

The neighbouring island of Alderney was intended to form a naval base for a squadron of torpedo boats during the close of the last century and a massive breakwater was built to enclose Braye Harbour on its north coast. The onslaught of the Atlantic has made upkeep of this long stone bulwark immensely costly and part of it has been irrecoverably lost. Braye Harbour is dominated by the elegant white tower of the lighthouse on Quenard Point, built in 1912 as part of a general improvement which included the construction of Point Robert. Like Sark and Casquets, it was occupied by the Germans during the last war and the whole island of Alderney is still littered with the ugly excrescences of Nazi concrete with which Hitler constructed his vaunted Atlantic Wall. These hideous buildings, constructed by slave-labour, retain an unpleasant and haunting atmosphere.

Many of the aids to navigation through the Channel Islands are provided by the local authorities. Apart from the lighthouses described, Trinity House maintains some buoys here, most notably around the Plateau des Minquiers. "The Minkies", as it is colloquially known, is best seen on a glass-calm summer's day at low water, when the extent of the reefs can be observed. It resembles nothing so much as row after row of black teeth, a terrible, forbidding death-trap of a place, penetrated by lobster and crab fishermen who know their way about, and a few intrepid yachtsmen who, I suspect, have never seen the place in a gale. Hammond Innes set much of his splendid story *The Wreck of the "Mary Deare"* on Les Minquiers and its dreary desolation was well chosen for such a yarn.

There are no Trinity House stations on Jersey but the locally run automatic lighthouse of La Corbière on Jersey's west coast is of passing interest. It was built in 1874 and was Britain's first concrete lighthouse. Round it steam the ferries that maintain communication between St Helier and the mainland of Britain and it is an appropriate headland from which to take our departure, both metaphorically and navigationally, from the Channel Islands and return northwards to England and the mysterious geological formation west of Portland Bill.

From Bridport to Portland the eastern sweep of Lyme Bay is composed of eighteen miles of shingle. This extraordinary bank of stones is no mere haphazard deposit. At Bridport the stones are no larger than peas, the beach no more than 170 yards wide, no more than 25 feet high and extending seawards to a depth of no more than six fathoms. At Portland the stones are the size of a man's fist, the bank has increased to a width of 200 yards, the height to 40 feet and it extends seawards to a depth of eight fathoms. Theories attempting to solve the conundrum of Chesil Beach are confounded by experiment. There does not seem to be any constant eastern or western movement. Pieces of broken brick, unequal in size, are rounded into pebbles and deposited in places appropriate to their size. Similarly, limestone pebbles coming from the Isle of Portland are found near Bridport, whilst material coming from the west goes the other way. Many have tried to account for this phenomenon, including the rather unlikely figure of Baden-Powell, but all that seems clear is that the beach is the result of highly complex and variable combinations of wind, wave and tide.

Chesil Beach lies on a clay bed and has impounded a salt-lagoon behind it, known as The Fleet. Tidal movement within The Fleet is affected through Weymouth to the east, although in bad weather considerable quantities of water are thrown over Chesil Beach. In 1824, for instance, the schooner *Ebenezer* was thrown bodily over the beach into The Fleet by a gale-engrossed high tide. Although a "non-static" geological formation, Chesil Beach formed one of the most formidable lee shores in the days of sail. A ship might well find herself embayed here, unable to tack to windward and weather Portland Bill. Relatively deep water extends close inshore and old-fashioned anchors with hemp cables could not always hold against an onshore gale. A captain might, if he and his crew were skilful enough, execute a club-haul. This was a desperate manoeuvre in which a ship pulled her head round forcibly by dropping an anchor and holding on the cable when it was judged sufficient had run out to enable the anchor to bite into the sea-bed. As the vessel's bow came round the sails were hauled in, the cable cut and the ship stood to seawards as close to the wind as she could. There were, however, so many things that could go wrong that it was rarely used. If the anchor failed to hold, the ship drove helplessly to leeward; if the anchor held too well, the ship might be jerked right round head to wind and held "in irons", unable to pay off on either tack and completely out of control. All depended on everything being in the right place at the right time, a proven remedy in a seamanship primer, but in practice far from easy. Captain Hayes of HMS *Magnificent* executed such a manoeuvre in the Basque Roads, France, in 1814 and was ever afterwards referred to as "Magnificent" Hayes.

Less fortunate was Admiral Christian in the New Year of 1796. He sailed for the West Indies with a large expeditionary force, intending to seize the French sugar islands. In the Chops of the Channel the fleet met a strong gale. Contemporary accounts tell of the chaos as the ships got foul of each other and became damaged and unmanageable. The warships and troop transports "went to the devil". Many foundered and seven ships ended up on Chesil Beach.

The town of Bridport, at the western end of Chesil Beach, was for centuries a centre of the rope-making industry. Hemp was first manufactured into rope there by the Romans and the industry survived until the last rope-walk was closed in 1970. The slang expression "Bridport dagger" referred to the hangman's noose and was used euphemistically. To have a friend or relative "stabbed by a Bridport dagger", was marginally less shameful than admitting he had been hanged!

After Bridport the coast rises again, sweeping west and south past Lyme Regis and on into Devon. At Golden Gap the cliffs rise to 626 feet, the highest point in southern England, but they are subject to sudden and dramatic collapse. In 1811 a rock-fall took place at Black Ven, revealing to twelve-year-old Mary Anning the skeleton of an ichthyosaurus, a primitive porpoise. The subsequent interest in her discovery stimulated the study of prehistory. A few miles south-

Point Robert lighthouse on the island of Sark.

west, at Downland Cliffs, occurred the greatest recorded landslip in England when an estimated eight million tons of water-logged chalk fell away with a mighty roar on Christmas Day 1839. Beer Head is the most southerly chalk headland in England; to the west the chalk is replaced by crumbling red sandstone. Pierced by river mouths at Axmouth, Sidmouth and Budleigh Salterton, the coast is steep to, the red cliffs spectacularly beautiful and, in their dissolution, they produce some striking formations such as the sheer stacks in Ladram Bay.

The estuary of the River Exe marks the westward extension of the newer rocks of eastern England. Roughly, a line drawn between the Exe and the Tees separates the older, igneous rocks of the west, Wales and the north-west from the sedimentary deposits of the south and east. As a general rule, the land west of this diagonal is higher and the coast begins to assume a different aspect. Except in very localized river estuaries and with a few exceptions in the Bristol Channel, sandbanks and shoals are supplanted by rocks and reefs as the principal offshore dangers. Rock lighthouses become more frequent, buoys less so, since a rock may be marked by a single buoy whereas a shoal may need several. On the whole the seabed is much deeper and the fifty-metre contour runs much closer to the coast. Both the Exe and the Teign are flooded river valleys. Their mouths are

The north coast of Alderney is dominated by the
elegant tower of the lighthouse on Quenard Point.

encumbered by sandbanks which need marking. In the case of the Exe, a special buoy design has to be employed to enable the seamark to remain upright during strong tides.

Great red cliffs rise behind Dawlish as the coast swings southward to form the two promontories of Hope's Nose and Berry Head. These two headlands are hard Devonian rock between which the Permo-triassic beds have been cut into to form the fine and magnificent anchorage beaches of Torbay. Used for centuries as a shelter from south-westerly gales, Torbay was of particular importance during the long Napoleonic War with France, providing shelter and victuals to the great fleet Britain was compelled to maintain blockading the French navy in Brest. It is of equal importance today, being used by very large tankers bringing crude oil from the Middle East. These huge ships anchor and transfer some of their cargo into smaller (though still pretty big) vessels. This lightens them and enables them to negotiate the shallow water of the eastern Channel and Dover Strait. Even so, it is often necessary for these great ships to "tide up Channel", riding the wave of high-water as they move eastwards to avoid grounding. The environmental pollution that would result if a disaster occurred to one of these ships would be catastrophic, so the operation of lightening them is a delicate one. The inherent risks of pollution are well understood by the tanker crews and stringent precautions are taken.

Torbay was the nearest Napoleon himself ever came to landing in Britain. Although a prisoner on board HMS *Bellerophon*, to whose captain he had surrendered at Rochefort, he made a conquest of sorts over the populace who flocked in their thousands to catch a glimpse of "Boney", the bogey-man of Europe for a generation. Mothers who had scared their children with tales of his baby-eating habits, saw a portly, sallow man staring down at them from the battleship's quarterdeck, now a rather pathetic figure. Refusing his request to live quietly in England, the Tory government, encouraged by Tsar Alexander, King Frederick William of Prussia, the Emperor of Austria and the terrified Bourbons, ordered his exile on the island of St Helena. He was transferred to HMS *Northumberland* and taken to the South Atlantic where, so modern forensic scientists believe, he was slowly poisoned by Bourbon agents under the nose of his British guards.

Torbay is enclosed at its southern end by Berry Head, a high cliffy headland surmounted by a squat automatic lighthouse. Due to its great natural height and in order to avoid occlusion by mist, the lantern is almost level with the ground, surrounded by green railings and grazing sheep. The marking of Berry Head is vital to guide ships into the shelter of Torbay and to indicate the pilot station of Brixham where pilots may be engaged to assist vessels through the Channel, the Dover Strait and on into the North Sea. The little port of Brixham is famous for its fishing fleets, and for a period in the late eighteenth century it was the premier fishing port in Britain. To carry out their difficult and dangerous work, local boat-builders developed a particularly handsome 75-foot-long, ketch-rigged sailing vessel, powerful enough to trawl offshore in all but the worst weather and reaching the height of its efficiency during the last century. They continued to be built into the present century, the design migrating to Lowestoft as the fish-stocks moved. Today only a few remain; the best known, the *Provident*, is preserved by a trust and can be seen cruising the south coast during the summer months.

It was at Brixham that William of Orange and his supporters landed on Sunday, 5 November 1688. Cruising offshore, William heard the church bells ringing and assuming that this was in his honour, he ordered a landing – and was well received by the population. Tucked inconspicuously round the corner from Berry Head, lies the beautiful entrance to Dartmouth Harbour. Heavily wooded, the land is steep and rocky to the water's edge, the river making a sharp bend as it breaks through into the sea. Both sides of this narrow and lovely entrance are fortified and, in the past, a great chain or boom could be hauled across the entrance. The original castle was built by the Yorkist Edward IV and then much improved by Henry VIII who added the defensive boom. Once through the narrows, Dartmouth opens out, a glorious basin surrounded by hills and full of small boats and fishing vessels, brightly painted. In 1863 an old wooden battleship was anchored off the town to form an officers' training ship. The present Britannia Royal Naval College takes its name from the old vessel that it was built to supersede. Dartmouth's naval connections are indeed ancient. In the Middle Ages crusaders sailed for the Holy Land from Bear's Cove; in 1588 nine ships left to engage the Spanish Armada. In 1620 the pilgrim ships *Speedwell* and *Mayflower*, the latter under the command of Christopher Jones of Harwich, with those dissenters on board who had been imprisoned briefly at Boston, put into Dartmouth to repair storm damage, before finally taking their departure for the New World from Plymouth. More recently, over 400 landing craft left the estuary in June 1944, bound for the Normandy Beaches and intent on breaching Hitler's Atlantic Wall. Rehearsals of the landing were held on the long stretch of Slapton Sands that back Start Bay.

Considering the shelter that may be obtained in Start Bay or Torbay, it is surprising that a lighthouse was not built on Start Point during the heyday of speculative private ownership. It was in fact 1836 when James Walker undertook this important work. The architecture reflects something of the Gothic flavour then fashionable, but it is the date of its building that is significant, for this was, of course, the year that Trinity House took over all the lighthouses in private ownership. In fact, few individuals had built lighthouses in the West Country and there was a great dearth of them, so when it acquired its monopoly Trinity House set about remedying this. Originally the establishment at Start Point consisted of two lights, one revolving to seawards, the other fixed over the Skerries Bank. The optic was designed by Alan Stevenson, the Scots engineer of the Northern Lighthouse Board, a reflection on the earlier deficiencies of Trinity House. A fog signal was added to the lights in 1865 and the housing of this was recently the victim of a landslip in the mica schists forming the headland.

The South Hams of Devon terminate in Prawle Point, swinging west again, the cliffs and headlands alternating with the flooded river valleys form some of the most beautiful yachting harbours and cruising grounds in the country. Across the entrance to Salcombe lies Bolt Head, under whose brow the Finnish four-masted barque *Herzogin Cecilie* ran ashore and was wrecked in 1936. Built in Germany at the beginning of the present century for the Norddeutscher-Lloyd Line as a training ship, she was capable of carrying over 4,000 tons of cargo. She was sold after the German defeat of 1918 and acquired by the Finnish ship-owner Gustav Erikson who salvaged some of the finest commercial sailing ships then in existence and for a few short years ran them successfully on the grain run from Australia. The best record of one of these last voyages under sail is related by Eric Newby who was an apprentice on another Erikson ship, the *Moshulu*, in *The Last*

Grain Race. The River Erme debouches into the western corner of Bigbury Bay and at Yealm Head the estuary of the River Yealm is dominated by the great slanting red rock known as the Mewstone, the home of sea-birds and the eastern limit of the gunnery range at HMS *Cambridge*. This "stone frigate" reminds the coasting mariner that round Wembury Point lies Plymouth, western base of the

James Walker started to build this tower at Start Point for Trinity House in 1836.

Royal Navy since Drake abandoned his famous game of bowls to sail west, winkle the Spanish out of their anchorage off Falmouth and chase them up the Channel in 1588.

Lord Howe, for many years commander of the Channel Fleet, said that Plymouth would prove the graveyard of the Royal Navy, so dangerous was the Sound as an anchorage. Plymouth is a great double ria, formed in the Ice Age. It has steep-to sides and a relatively flat bottom, covered in fine sand. Two rivers and several minor streams flow into it, making it a natural harbour of considerable size. But the main anchorage suitable for wooden warships ready to work out into the open sea was exposed to the south, often subject to heavy swells that rolled into it and lethal in bad weather. This was Howe's chief objection to using the Sound rather than Torbay where he might have had the services of the adjacent dockyard to repair his fleet.

Several vessels were lost in the Sound, the most spectacular disaster occurring during the Napoleonic War when the Indiaman *Dutton* parted her cable and drove ashore under the Hoe and rolled her three masts overboard. This took place in full view of hundreds of the townsfolk and a daring rescue attempt was made under the direction of Captain Sir Edward Pellew. One of Britain's most dashing frigate captains, Pellew enhanced his already dazzling reputation for courage and fearlessness by rigging a line from the shore, crossing to the stricken ship and coolly supervising the evacuation. That Pellew was on his way to an official dinner and wore full-dress uniform including his sword, only increased the drama! Later becoming an admiral, Pellew was made a peer for his part in reducing Algiers in 1816 after the failure of negotiations with the Dey to free Christian slaves.

Apprehensions for the safety of the fleet were eventually allayed when, after the Napoleonic Wars, the breakwater was built, transforming the Sound into the magnificent anchorage it now is. The breakwater is marked at its western end by an automatic acetylene-powered lighthouse maintained by Trinity House. On the Hoe above the Sound stands the upper two-thirds of John Smeaton's Eddystone lighthouse. It was removed when the present tower was built, as the rock on which it stood was thought to be undermined. An impressive municipal donation ensured Smeaton's achievement was preserved. The present lighthouse on the Eddystone is fully automatic and is monitored by telemetry at the Trinity House fog-signal station at Penlee Point.

Fourteen miles from the entrance to Plymouth and eight south of Rame Head, lies the Eddystone Reef. "Twenty-three rust red granite rocks . . . great ragged stones around which the sea constantly eddies, a great danger . . . for if any vessel makes too far to the south . . . she will be caught in the prevailing strong current and swept to her doom on these evil rocks." So wrote Christopher Jones, master of the *Mayflower* in the early seventeenth century, echoing a widespread fear. Over seventy years later, following successive petitions, William and Mary decreed that "having regard for the many gallant seamen who have perished round these dangerous rocks, these said captains, shipowners and merchants are agreed and willing to pay to the Corporation of Trinity House one penny a ton outward and . . . inward for the benefit of a warning light."

Lacking any kind of expertise in the matter, despite the recent construction of the lighthouse on St Agnes, the Elder Brethren were unable to comply. The fact was that *no one* possessed the experience to build a tower on such a remote, wave-swept rock. And it was not just expertise that was required, but vision, ingenuity and boundless confidence too, qualities not to be found among mariners with a lifetime's experience of the destructive power of the sea. None of the builders of early offshore lighthouses came from orthodox backgrounds. Henry Whiteside of the Smalls was an instrument maker, Robert Stevenson of the Bell Rock a copper "hammerman", but most extraordinary of all was the architect and builder of the first two lighthouses on the Eddystone, Henry Winstanley.

Brought up in the household of the Earl of Suffolk in which he served as a porter, Winstanley showed an early inventiveness. When Suffolk sold his house at Audley End to Charles II, Winstanley built one of his own between Audley End and Nell Gwyn's house at Newport. He appears to have travelled on the Continent and had just married, acquiring sufficient funds to put up a pretence of wealth. His house at Littlebury was an opulent establishment, deliberately made into a curiosity, stuffed with mechanical contrivances, trick devices, mirrors that caused illusions and so forth. It was known locally as "Winstanley's Wonders" and it did what its owner intended, attracting the notice of the libertine court and, as a consequence, the shillings of every curious person willing to travel and enjoy the discomfiture of Winstanley's sardonic and rather malevolent humour.

Winstanley continued to exercise his fertile imagination by marketing all manner of goods including "geographical playing cards", portraits of the country houses of gentlemen and a display of "Waterworkes" in Piccadilly. He attracted royal notice and obtained the sinecure of Clerk of the Works for Audley End, an appointment from which he may have gained some knowledge of building methods. By his fiftieth birthday Winstanley was well-known as a showman, an artist, inventor, publicity man, an illusionist, a conjuror, eccentric and a businessman. But he still hungered after true respectability and with his money purchased two ships to become a merchant and ship-owner. Almost immediately he lost both vessels on the Eddystone and, not content to accept his fate, he made some inquiries into the disasters. He discovered that royal sanction to build a lighthouse on the Eddystone was already two years old and that Trinity House had sold a lease to a Plymouth man who had done nothing about it. It began to dawn upon Winstanley that here was not merely a passport to the gentry, but an opportunity for true immortality. To his other accomplishments, Winstanley decided to add that of lighthouse engineer.

It is important to see Winstanley in his true light. From the most obscure origins he had worked his way up, driven by an ambition to succeed and perhaps to ridicule the frivolous world he found himself a part of. If he managed to build the Eddystone lighthouse, his name would not merely be associated with transient nine-day wonders. Even the prospect of failure had something heroic about it. His imagination was captivated by the whole idea as much as his anger had been roused by the financial loss of his ships. Whatever the outcome of the project, society would no longer call Winstanley "an adventurer", or so he hoped.

The Eddystone comprises three ridges of granitoid gneiss (the only other example of it being found at Prawle Point) formed with a roughly sloping western face and a vertical eastern face. The prevailing westerly winds create seas and swells which roll up the western slope. When the wind freshens from the east, sharp, short and dangerous waves smash against the vertical face upon that side. The situation is further confused by the circular motion of the tides as described in 1839: "where the strongest eddy of the bay (the vast bight between the Lizard and Prawle Point) holds conflict with the tide around the Lizard.'' In other words, the disturbance of the true run of the tidal stream east/west is confused by the southern salient of the headland made up of Prawle Point, Bolt Head and Start Point. Much local turbulence is, of course, generated by the configuration of the reef itself. At all events, as its name suggests, the Eddystone Reef was a constant danger due to the effect of the tides, not just in bad weather.

Winstanley decided that the westernmost rock offered the best site for a tower. A careful study of the tides encouraged him to attempt the transport of heavy stone blocks, an incredibly difficult business. The short voyage alone, under oars and sail, might take many hours in a deeply laden boat. Winstanley and his workmen could only work in the summer months and for the first two years they were unable to leave anything on the rocks that was not fixed and had to transport all their tools backwards and forwards. Summer gales and the swells generated by distant storms hampered them without remission, yet in four years the lighthouse was built.

In the summer of 1696 Winstanley had a dozen holes bored in the rock. Into these he intended to fit iron stanchions. After an eight-hour passage to the Eddystone, it was as much as his men could do to strike the hard gneiss. They were often swept by waves and constantly spray-soaked. Winstanley now added leadership to his impressive list of talents. He built up in his men an insensate hatred of the stubborn rock; he wheedled, he cajoled, he joked. He did everything his ingenious mind could invent to keep the picks chipping at the rock to excavate those twelve holes. By late October Winstanley's persistance had won. The iron stanchions were bedded into the rock with molten lead. The following summer the stone blocks were put in place, levelling off the slope. Precise details of the work are not known but Winstanley now had other problems. Interested in his project, the Admiralty had ordered HMS *Terrible* to patrol the area to protect the workmen from the French with whom we were again at war. But, for some reason, the naval ship was absent from her station one day and a French privateer descended on the rock, taking Winstanley prisoner.

Winstanley's fame had spread across the Channel. Louis XIV in a characteristic speech, declaring that he ''was at war with England not humanity'', summoned Winstanley to Versailles and was charmed by the Englishman. The seductions of the court of the Sun King must have been considerable and it says much for Winstanley's dedication that within a fortnight, despite offers of employment in France, he was once more on English soil having been released and showered with gifts by King Louis. By the end of the season, despite this adventure, there was on the rock ''a solid body or kind of rough pillar twelve foot high and fourteen foot diameter''. In the third year the base was enlarged and the octagonal masonry tower rose in tiers, first a store-room, then a living apartment. Once this was completed, the workmen could live on site. In June they settled to spend the first night on the rock. A gale blew up and for eleven days no boat could approach but they, and the tower, survived. Above this prefabricated wooden upper floors were added, greatly embellished and decorated, surmounted by a pretentious weather vane. On 14 November 1698 Winstanley climbed up and lit the candelabra. The good people of Plymouth rushed to the Hoe to see the new wonder of the world on their own doorsteps. Winstanley had lit the Eddystone and built the first true rock lighthouse in the world.

The resentful sea immediately blew itself into a gale and it was five weeks before a boat took off Winstanley and his workmen, leaving the new keepers to attend the light. The following spring Winstanley returned to the house to examine it for weather damage. He found the cement used between the blocks of the base had been washed away and the family keeping the light told terrifying tales of how the tower shook when pounded by the sea. Undeterred, Winstanley undertook to strengthen and enlarge the tower. He encased the original base, covered all the joints with iron bands and raised the tower height from 80 to 120 feet, achieving all this in a single summer! Winstanley's own drawing of his second lighthouse was taken by the London print makers and became a best-seller. His reputation was made, his fame national.

But the voice of the sceptics was now heard; after the achievement the debunking. The tales of the keepers were enlarged by those of the workmen. The octagonal design was all wrong, the foundation was too weak and, worst of all, the extravagant decoration was an affront to the severe, puritan God that still dwelt in the hearts of the citizens of Plymouth. Perhaps they had had enough of the flamboyant Henry Winstanley. Winstanley hit back, declaring publicly that he wished for nothing more than to be inside his lighthouse during "the greatest storm there ever was".

Fate took him at his word. On the night of 26/27 November 1703, as we have seen, the whole of England was swept by the greatest storm ever recorded. It was the culmination of a fortnight of Atlantic gales that were already being claimed a record in living memory. The anchorages of Britain were full of sheltering vessels, including Admiral Beaumont's squadron in The Downs. An anxious Winstanley assembled his workmen and, in the lull that was thought to have signalled the end of the bad weather, he set out to inspect the lighthouse for damage. The afternoon of Friday 26 November was calm and the nation went to bed, hoping that its chimney pots were safe again.

Winstanley reached the Eddystone and, despite the residual ground swell, managed to scramble ashore and into the lighthouse. In the morning he would begin his inspection. Shortly before midnight the wind backed south-westerly and began to freshen very quickly. It passed gale force to whine with a terrifying roar, the masterwind that signalled the very end of the world as men knew it. It was a night of total darkness, a night of the new moon and spring tides, a night when only the reality of the wind-roar existed in the consciousness of men.

On land chimneys, trees, even the spire of Stowmarket church, crashed to the ground. Six college towers at Oxford were damaged, Queen Anne sought the shelter of a cellar and the Bishop of Bath and Wells and his wife were killed in bed by falling masonry. Tiles flew horizontally and buried themselves several inches in the sides of hills; birds died in heaps, church roofs were stripped of lead in seconds; windmills were blown to pieces and one cottage was lifted bodily and transported several yards. Rivers burst their banks and at Bristol the high spring tide caused thousands of pounds worth of damage to stored merchandise.

At sea the effects beggar description. The storm, at its worst in the small hours of the Saturday, veered into the north-west and then backed again, but by eight in the morning it was all over. Daniel Defoe, who lived through the night, estimated that some 150 ships were lost and that 8,000 seamen had been drowned. So too had Henry Winstanley, his workmen and keepers. At daybreak on 27 November all that stood on the Eddystone were a few bent stanchions of iron. No bodies were ever recovered.

But Winstanley had shown that it was after all possible to build on the Eddystone. The lease passed to a certain Captain Lovatt, whose patent was taken up by John Rudyerd, a London silk-mercer. He was also a man of scientific inclination who had designed a tower on ship-building principles with the aid of two shipwrights from Woolwich, named Smith and Norcutt. They selected a conical shape made of huge wooden planks into which they packed stone weights, relying on the timber joints used in the construction of ships to prove as useful in a lighthouse. Rudyerd also increased the number of bolts grouted into the rock from twelve to thirty-six major and two hundred minor insertions. These bolts were secured with wedges and molten pewter. The tower rose rapidly and its main drawback was not on account of any weakness, but due to the heavy timber framework of the lantern obscuring much of the light. The first light was shown on 28 July 1708, less than five years after Winstanley's death. Although the base of the tower was attacked by ship-worm, Rudyerd's tower survived until 1755 when the candles in the lantern set fire to the wooden framework. The flames spread quickly and the keepers gave up the attempt to extinguish them and fled out on to the rock. Fortunately it was a calm night and they were picked up by a fishing boat. One of them, Henry Hall, had swallowed some molten lead as he looked upwards in escaping from the fire. His death a few days later at the age of eighty-four was attributed to his extreme age and delayed shock, but a nugget of lead, over seven ounces in weight, was found in his stomach and may be seen today in the Royal Scottish Museum at Edinburgh.

The lessee, desirous of swiftly re-establishing his source of income, applied to the President of the Royal Society, Lord Macclesfield, for a suitable person to undertake the rebuilding. (Rudyerd had long since disappeared without trace, an example followed by Henry Hall's fellow lighthouse keeper once he got ashore!) Macclesfield recommended John Smeaton, who accepted the commission and produced a design for a stone tower based upon the graceful curve of the bole of an oak tree. Smeaton considered this would dissipate the destructive force of the swells. He began work in August 1756 and saved much time by anchoring a store and accommodation vessel close to the rock in good weather. To enable finances to be raised to fund the work, Trinity House agreed to anchor a lightvessel nearby.

Unlike Winstanley, Smeaton prepared the rock itself by levelling it in steps and cutting dovetails in the gneiss. The blocks forming the tower base were secured to these, each having been tested for fit ashore before shipping out to the rock to avoid time-wasting alterations on site. This practice, obvious with hindsight and ever afterwards adopted, was innovative at the time. Smeaton's plan was to make the lighthouse an almost integral part of the rock itself, by using the skills of the mason's craft combined with the sheer weight of the stones. He was considerably annoyed by the activities of naval press-gangs, busy forcing men into the Royal Navy during the Seven Years' War but work proceeded apace. In December 1757 the neighbouring lightvessel was driven off station but the base of the tower had been completed. It was first illuminated on 16 October 1759, using candles. Smeaton's tower was eighty feet high, a prototype for every succeeding rock lighthouse in the world and while the original light was not particularly effective, this does not detract from his design. A modest and engaging man, Smeaton never sought profit from his skills, claiming that "two guineas for a full day's work" was sufficient and that work was its own reward. "The abilities of the individual are a debt due to the common stock of public well being," he wrote. What a broadside to fire at materialism! James Watt called him "Father" Smeaton and the railway builder George Stephenson described him as "a very great man".

Although Smeaton exceeded Winstanley in the strength of his design, he failed to elevate his light as far. In 1878 it was decided to remedy this, at the same time as reports indicated the rock on which Smeaton had built was being undermined by the sea. A new tower was designed and supervised by James Douglass, son of Nicholas Douglass who introduced the vertical dovetailing to Les Hanois that was the logical follow-up to Smeaton's horizontal binding. This completely united every stone in the entire structure and was employed by James Douglass in the last Eddystone. Douglass was also greatly aided by the employment of a specially constructed steam-ship, the *Hercules*. On board *Hercules* each individual stone block, pre-cut ashore, sat on a wheeled bogie in her holds. Over her stern a heavy steel gantry had been built and *Hercules* arrived daily at the rock, weather permitting, to make fast to a specially laid mooring buoy. As she moored, a heavy wire was picked up and set up over the stern gantry to form the main wire of an aerial runway. Each block was hoisted out of the hold and trundled aft on rails until it could be hoisted under the wire to be hauled ashore by steam winches. The tower was built in record time, on a rock adjacent to Smeaton's. It weighs 4,668 tonnes and consists of 2,171 granite blocks. On 18 May 1882 the powerful new optic with its polished fresnel lenses shone out from the new tower. In his original estimate Douglass had reckoned it would take five years to build, at a cost of £78,000. In the event it was completed in three and a half years for £59,250. In June Douglass received a knighthood from Queen

Victoria for his services.

Shortly afterwards Smeaton's tower was taken down (an operation supervised by Sir James's son, William, and one which nearly cost him his life), to be erected on its present site on Plymouth Hoe where it dominates the harbour. Since that time Douglass's tower on the reef has been altered by the addition of a helicopter pad over the top of the lantern. Inside it has undergone a greater revolution. In July 1981 the light was doused, being replaced once again by a lightvessel. The inside of the tower was ripped out and the station was fitted with the latest electronically monitored automatic systems to provide its light and other services. Today there are no lighthouse keepers on the Eddystone to sleep with the mermaids as in the vulgar old song. Twelve months after closing down and on the centenary of its commissioning, Sir James Douglass's lighthouse re-opened as a fully automatic rock light. The lightvessel was towed away and the lighthouse was left alone to shine its warning over "the twenty-three rust red granite rocks" of the Eddystone Reef.

CHAPTER SEVEN
THE CORNISH SALIENT

Hartland Point.

Cornwall stabs south-west, a gigantic, arrow-headed salient. Separated from its tip at Land's End by some twenty-odd miles, lies the outwork of the Isles of Scilly, a ravelin to break the Atlantic's onslaught. Cornwall's battle with the ocean is a losing one, despite the hardness of her ancient carboniferous rocks. Everything testifies to this slow decay: the rounded granite outcrops on the cliff-tops, the windswept and stunted trees, the coastal waterfalls which tell of abbreviated rivers, the thin soil and, above all the coast of broken rock. Close inspection of Cornwall's magnificent cliffs reveals this process of disintegration. There are fissures, faults and cracks, the tiny intrusions of roots grasping at the minuscule pockets of nourishment briefly afforded by the breakdown of the rock. Cornwall's north coast is bleak, the south more tractable, being pierced by the folds of valleys and river beds that flow south and east to the sea, their ancient glacial valleys submerged to form rias. Rocks and islands cling close to the shore and everywhere deep water runs close up to the cliffs. In the main, the coastal villages of Cornwall such as Looe and Polperro huddle in the river valleys, round the small harbours that nature or man's artifice have made.

Fowey is a small ria into which quite large ships run to load china clay. Very similar to Dartmouth, Fowey attracted the notice of King Henry VIII who fortified the entrance and fitted a boom. The men of Fowey, known as "Fowey Gallants", were notorious in the sixteenth and seventeenth centuries for their lawlessness. If a war was not on hand to distract their restless spirits, they were not above aggravating a little local bad feeling or plundering passing ships, irrespective of nationality. Like its neighbours, Fowey enjoyed a certain prosperity from fishing and boat-building, particularly in the last century. The literary critic and author, Sir Arthur Quiller-Couch was mayor of the town and used it, as he did other places in the locality, for background in his stories. Another local literary figure is the novelist Daphne Du Maurier, whose house on Gribben Head at Menabilly was the model for Manderley in her best known novel, *Rebecca*.

A short distance from Menabilly stands the Gribben Head daymark, a tall stone tower painted brightly in alternating red and white bands. It was erected by Trinity House in 1832 to enable fishing vessels to lay their courses for home for, although the coast is high, from a distance it is comparatively featureless, the narrow entrance to Fowey being difficult to see until fairly close. At St Austell the coast swings south, a succession of small bays each with its village, as far as Dodman Point. This is a high sedimentary point, the landfall made by the man o' war in *Spanish Ladies*. It bears no lighthouse but is surmounted by a great cross raised by a local rector in 1896, "in the firm hope of the second coming of our

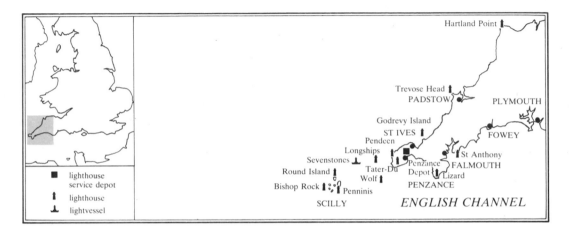

Lord Jesus Christ". Following its dedication, he spent the night on his knees praying for the souls of wrecked seamen, unlike his parishioners, who usually prayed for a "good wreck".

There is a westward trend to the coast across the wide sweep of Veryan Bay between the Dodman and the promontory of Nare Head. These hard igneous points almost always produce off-lying dangers (Cannis Rock off Gribben Head, for instance, which is marked by a buoy) and off Nare Head the Whelps lie awash off the islet of Gull Rock. Another bay sweeps west, then south to Greeb Point which is of volcanic ash and flanks St Anthony's Head. St Anthony's forms the eastern part of the entrance to Falmouth Harbour. Ships entering the haven have to lay their courses close to the St Anthony side to avoid the Black Rock below Pendennis opposite. Formed by the flooding of a number of converging river valleys, Falmouth harbour is surrounded by green hills and woodland, one of the loveliest natural harbours in the country. Important from earliest times as a haven of refuge, it was protected by Henry VIII who built two castles, one high on Pendennis Head, commanding the outer approaches and Falmouth Bay, the second lower down, its guns commanding the narrow entrance to the harbour itself. Royalist Pendennis resisted the forces of Parliament during a protracted siege in 1646, holding out from March to August, only two days less than the Civil

The Sevenstones lightvessel marks the granite reef to the west of Land's End which lies awash at low water. The station is the most exposed of any around the British Isles.

Wolf Rock at sunset. The lighthouse was built in 1869.

War record set at Raglan. Over a quarter of the defenders were sick and although Fairfax was unable to carry the castle by storm, its governor, Colonel Arundel of Trerice, surrendered on 17 August. Built eight years before Pendennis, St Mawes was completed in 1640 and is generally considered the best of Henry's coastal forts. Its design of a central bastion supported by three semi-circular bastions in a seaward orientated clover-leaf, was not designed to resist attack from the land. The castle surrendered to Fairfax immediately on his arrival in March 1646. Falmouth marked its loyalty to the Royalist cause after the Restoration of Charles II, by dedicating the new parish church to King Charles the Martyr.

The growing communication with the thirteen American colonies and Canada during the eighteenth century made Falmouth the point of departure and arrival for the trans-Atlantic mail packets. For more than a century and a half, between 1688 and 1852, these fast yacht-like sailing ships with their distinctive ensigns and pennants bearing the post-horn device of the Royal Mail, maintained as regular a service as the winds allowed. Frequently involved in bloody little actions with French and American privateers, these lightly armed ships distinguished themselves in a number of sea-fights in the long wars of the eighteenth century. Most were locally owned and on a long term charter to the Post Office. In 1852 the service from Falmouth was discontinued in favour of a steamer service from Southampton. In its heyday the packet service, like the mail-coach, was a synonym for speed, and post-chaises and mail coaches were kept in instant readiness at Falmouth to meet the little ships. In November 1805 Lieutenant Lapenotière of HM Schooner *Pickle* landed there with the news of Trafalgar. He had left his ship at 9.45 on the morning of the 4th and arrived at the Admiralty with Collingwood's despatch at 1 a.m. on the 6th, having changed horses nineteen times.

Falmouth has an extensive commercial port, including a drydock facility, and supports a small inshore fishing fleet of diesel boats and the last fishery worked exclusively by sailing boats. The River Fal oyster dredgers are lovely gaff-rigged cutters that owe their continued existence to the need to preserve the oyster-stocks from the dangers of over-fishing. Trawling under sail maintains the delicate balance between supply and demand. A fine sight under any conditions, these craft are particularly impressive when sailed in competition during their annual races.

Falmouth's entrance is marked by a large beacon on the Black Rock. This was first indicated by a great flag, replaced by a beacon in the eighteenth century. The present lighthouse on St Anthony's Head was built in 1835 and still displays an occulting light, coloured red over the Manacles Rocks to the south of the harbour entrance. Extending nearly a mile off Manacle Point on the eastern extreme of the Lizard peninsula, this reef has claimed many hundreds of lives. In 1855 the emigrant transport *John* ran on to them with the loss of 196 souls and in 1898 the steamer *Mohegan* broke up on them with the loss of over 100 people. Bringing home troops, many of them wounded, from the Peninsular War in 1809,

HM Armed Transport *Despatch* hit the Manacles and went to pieces. Within hours the eighteen-gun brig *Primrose* suffered the same fate. The loss of the *Despatch* forms the background to one of Quiller-Couch's most eerie tales of the supernatural, *The Roll Call on the Reef*.

The high cliffs and secluded bays that form the east coast of the Lizard are beautiful in any conditions. The Lizard is largely composed of serpentine, but there are also schists and gabbro near the village of Coverack. Although in the lee of the prevailing winds, the remorseless process of erosion goes on, exemplified at Cadgwith where a great hole known as the Devil's Frying Pan has been formed by the collapse of a cave roof. The Lizard is the most southerly headland in England, thrusting out into the warm, damp air of the westerlies. On its eastern side it is noted for the profusion of its flora and in under an hour it is possible to see grasses, gorse, nettles and thistles, hartstongue, wild carrot, foxgloves, thrift, sheep's bit, penny-wort, lesser spearwort, common mouse-ear, sea-campion, white stonecrop and kidney vetch. The area is also known for its rarer plants such as Cornish Heath, wild asparagus, domed sea-carrot, western clover, tree mallow and hairy dyer's greenweed. This fertile land was owned in the early seventeenth century by Sir John Killigrew of Arwenack House, Falmouth. In partnership with his cousin, Lord Dorchester, Killigrew proposed to Trinity House that the Lizard was an ideal site for a lighthouse and that this would discourage the local inhabitants from showing false lights to induce shipwrecks. In 1619 Trinity House was not in favour, arguing that a lighthouse there would expose the coast to an enemy and that, as there was deep water round the point, a lighthouse was not really necessary. However, Killigrew secured a patent directly from the Duke of Buckingham, who was then the Lord High Admiral and able to grant one without consulting Trinity House. The patent entitled Killigrew and his partner to build their lighthouse, maintain it as a charity and collect voluntary contributions for its upkeep. This can scarcely have been exactly what Killigrew wanted in terms of financial return, but at least he had permission to build. He went ahead and soon found the matter

> far more Troublesom than I expected for the inhabitants near think they suffer . . . They affirm I take away God's Grace from them. Their English meaning is that they now shall receive no more benefit by shipwreck . . . They have been so long used to reap by the Calamity of the Ruin of Shipping as they claim it Hereditary, and hourly complain on me. Custom breeds strange ills . . .

In December 1619 the work was complete, though Killigrew found the light expensive to maintain. The voluntary contributions failed to come in and he strove to get the same terms as the owner of Dungeness, continually complaining of his difficulties. More ships were lost when the light was briefly extinguished, to the great joy of the locals because "I assure your Lordship that most of the houses near the Lizard are built with the ruins of ships." But in 1623 King Charles I decreed that "the lighthouse should remain a lighthouse for ever on that coast". Trinity House eagerly supported all complaints about its inefficiency, maintaining that an imperfectly kept light was worse than no light at all. In the end Killigrew ran out of money, the light was extinguished and the tower fell derelict.

This pathetic state of affairs lasted for some time, despite the king's decree. A near contemporary account of navigational conditions with particular reference to the Lizard was given by the distinguished naval officer, Sir William Monson: "It is most fit," he wrote, "seamen should be furnished with as many other helps as can be devised ... There is no man that hath lain tossing at sea some time but will be glad to make the land, for the good landfall is the principal thing to find coming for our coast." He goes on to describe Cavendish's predicament at the end of his circumnavigation of the globe (1586 to 1588 and the third undertaken following Magellan and Drake): "I remember Mr Cavendish, in his return voyage about the world, falling in with our Channel, somewhat short of the Lizard, he was taken with so great a storm that he could not make the land, and hath confessed to me, he endured more hazard and trouble in two nights upon our coast than in his long navigation ..." But no light appeared on the Lizard for more than a century until an application was made in 1848 by a Richard Farish. Trinity House insisted on Farish obtaining a petition and during the collection of signatures, Farish died. The matter proceeded, however, being taken up by Thomas Fonnereau and three years later two Elder Brethren travelled to the Lizard to survey the site at Fonnereau's expense. The outcome was, as we have seen, a decision to build twin towers to distinguish it from the lighthouse at St Agnes. The two towers were built without further delay and lit on 23 August 1752. Responsibility for the fires (thought to have been partially sheltered behind glass) lay with an overlooker whose house was constructed half-way between the towers. He lay at night on a couch, able to view each fire through specially made windows. When the keepers relaxed their efforts on the bellows, the overlooker reminded them of their duties with a blast on a cow-horn!

From this period Trinity House's attitude changed rapidly and in 1812 spent £5,000 on the virtual rebuilding of the two light towers and the installation of new optics. From this point the history of the Lizard is fairly straightforward. The reduction to a single tower occurred with the fitting of a revolving light and today the powerful electric optic has a nominal range of twenty-nine miles and the station is fitted with a racon and huge fog signal.

Between the Lizard and the Land's End peninsula the softer rocks of Mount's Bay are sedimentary and have succumbed to the onslaught of the ocean. Almost every cove has a tale of wreckage and treasure or smuggling. Many ships were wrecked in the bay, particularly near Mullion as they failed to weather the Lizard. In 1526 a Portuguese treasure ship, the *San Antonio*, was wrecked in Church Cove. Next door, in Dollar Cove, the coins from a Spanish vessel carrying specie which was wrecked in 1785 give the cove its name. A little further round the bay, another inlet was fortified by a smuggler who was said to resemble the King of Prussia, Frederick the Great, both in appearance and belligerence. Prussia Cove is supposed to have defied the revenue officers several times. Whatever the truth of this, Prussia Cove is where the battleship HMS *Warspite* ran ashore after breaking adrift from her tugs. She was being towed to the breakers in 1947 and although later refloated, she went ashore again at Marazion where she broke up in heavy weather. In 1807 the frigate *Anson* drove ashore in Mount's Bay and her crew perished in sight of the shore. One of the onlookers, Henry Trengrouse, was so affected that he devised a rocket-propelled line throwing apparatus which could carry a rescue line to a stricken vessel. From this idea came the invention of the breeches buoy.

Mount's Bay is dominated by the steep granite rock called St Michael's Mount. Its name is supposed to have been derived from an appearance of the archangel St Michael to some fishermen in AD 495. It also had ecclesiastical connections with Mont St Michel in Brittany before the Norman Conquest. It was first used for military purposes by Henry de Pomeroy who seized the place with a party of men disguised as monks during the reign of Richard I. The king was absent in the Holy Land and Pomeroy held the place in the name of Prince John. On Richard's return St Michael's Mount was retaken by a force under the Archbishop of Canterbury. During the Wars of the Roses it was captured by John De Vere, Earl of Oxford and a Lancastrian supporter who later joined Henry Tudor, Duke of Richmond, and led the vanguard against Richard III at Bosworth. The Mount was held for the king during the civil war and used as a prison. After 1660 it became a private house belonging to the St Aubyn family. Today it belongs to the National Trust.

Across the bay from St Michael's Mount lies the town of Penzance, formerly a major Trinity House station. Today its importance has declined. Built originally as the masonry working yard for the building of the Wolf Rock lighthouse, Penzance Depot now serves as a support base for engineering works on the Cornish lighthouses and for the helipad at Sennen, near Land's End, from which operations are conducted by helicopter to the Wolf Rock, Longships and Scilly lighthouses and the Sevenstones lightvessel. A small modern automatic concrete lighthouse was built in 1965 on Tater Du, a small headland near Land's End, in response to requests from fishermen. It overlooks the sea where, it is believed, the Penlee lifeboat *Solomon Browne* made its heroic rescue attempt to remove the crew of the disabled coaster *Union Star*. Both vessels and their crews vanished in appalling weather on the night of Saturday, 19 December 1981. Later the capsized wreck of the *Union Star* was washed ashore. Only a few pieces of wreckage were ever found belonging to the *Solomon Browne*. The violence of the seas as they meet and "wash-back" from the cliffs of Land's End is unimaginable. The energy that is thwarted by this mass of granite causes the release of immeasurable forces which fling masses of solid water high in the air. Air compressed in caves by the sea is capable of splitting granite and tearing boulders from cliffs and such "zawns" proliferate along this embattled coast. As the land retreats it leaves behind its wreckage, off-lying spurs and reefs of rock. South of Land's End lies the Runnelstone, marked by a buoy and some shore beacons, but the largest mass of this residue is the reef known as the Longships, off Land's End itself, gazed upon by thousands of summer visitors as they pose for photographs by the "First and Last House in England".

The Longships lighthouse stands on Carn Bras, the largest and most westerly rock. The first man to moot the idea of a light on such an exposed spot was an army officer, Lieutenant Henry Smith. By the late eighteenth century Trinity House was willing to encourage anyone with such enthusiasm. Smith was granted a patent and the tower was designed for him by Trinity House's own architect, Samuel Wyatt. The building seems to have been accomplished with remarkable ease. Starting in 1794, the work was completed the following year and it was lit on 29 September 1795. Masonry was chiselled and the fit of each block to its neighbour was tested ashore at Sennen, before shipping them out to the rock. Perhaps the seasons were mild, allowing the work to proceed at a cracking pace. But the tower had one disadvantage; it was too low. Made of granite, it had only three stories: a store and water reservoir, living space and lantern. Smith was not long left in possession. It seems he fell into debt, for in 1806 Stevenson interviewed him in the Fleet Prison. He was dispossessed by Trinity House who judged him a person "incapable of managing the concern". Trinity House took over management, remitting the profits to Smith's family. The keepers of the Longships had a pretty rough time. Their cooking, for instance, had to be done over the argand lights. They were, however, quite well paid, £30 per annum being generous for the period. They also had unusually good leave conditions, four men being employed in two monthly watches of two keepers.

The sea, "bounding and crashing and coiling in an anarchy of enormous power", in the words of John Ruskin, frequently swept the lantern and at times it must have been difficult to keep the Longships alight. Nevertheless it was 1873 before Sir James Douglass set about rebuilding. He constructed a tower adjacent to Smith's, taking the lantern up with the new tower so that it was never extinguished, and eventually demolishing the old building. In 1974 a helipad was added over the lantern and the now fully modernized lighthouse remains a manned station, showing an isophase light (one having equal periods of light and darkness), white to seaward, red over the rocks inshore.

Smith had earlier, tentatively suggested building a lighthouse on the Wolf Rock, but he soon realized this was utterly impracticable. About ten miles south, and a little west of Land's End, the Wolf Rock is even more isolated than the Eddystone, consisting of a single pinnacle, an outcrop of rare granite. Landing was always perilous for the rock was awash at most states of the tide and swept by waves even when the mean sea-level indicated it should be exposed. It was once said to have possessed a submarine cave and "chimney", which would fill with air and would then "howl" as water pressure drove the air out. Local wreckers are supposed to have filled in the hole with stones to prevent sailors hearing the noise and locating their position from it. In 1750 Trinity House proposed laying a bell buoy close to the rock but local fishermen maintained it would frighten the fish!

Smith's patent to build the Longships stated that he should also try to erect a beacon on the Wolf. He did manage to erect a staff with a whistle on the top to reproduce the howl of former days, but it was soon washed away. In 1835 Trinity House sent James Walker to erect a new beacon. Walker spent five years (during which he clocked up 302 hours of working time on the rock and spent a great deal of money) and finally succeeded in building a substantial beacon.

The success of Smeaton's Eddystone and the new availability of steam power to provide fast transit over to the building site, encouraged Walker to design a lighthouse on the Wolf. In order to prevent the cement being washed out of the interstices before it had set, Walker cut the upper surface of each of the lower course stones with a wide lip. The stone above fitted into the recess and the horizontal joint was protected. He first built a wide level platform, which remains today as the landing, upon which he fitted his stone-hoisting mast and derrick. Work began in 1861 and proceeded very slowly. Masonry was prepared at Penzance and the stones towed out in lighters by a tug. By the end of 1864 only thirty-seven stones of the second course were in place, but as the tower rose work became easier. It was finished on 19 July 1869 and lit early the next year. During the nineteenth century when relief of the keepers was carried out by ship, delays were frequent. It was possible to gauge the ground swell at the Wolf Rock by watching the rise and fall of the sea at Penzance. If more than two of the harbour steps covered and uncovered with the motion of the water, there would be no chance of a boat getting in to the rock. Even when a relief was possible, the boat never closed the rock physically, being held off by a system of ropes, while the men were transferred via a swinging derrick, lifted bodily like so many sacks. A relief was not considered "missed" until it was nineteen days overdue, when compensatory leave adjustments took place. Up to the nineteen-day deadline it was just hard luck, since both lots of men, those going off to the rock, and those coming ashore, were equally tied down. The introduction of the helicopter in 1969 has removed such injustices and all rock lighthouses have now been fitted with helipads over their lantern. These pads are made of perforated alloy to lessen wind resistance, their rims being sacrificial, designed to tear off rather than impose too great a strain on the tower.

Sixteen miles westward of Land's End, another series of rocks breaks surface. The Sevenstones is a reef of granite which lies awash at low water. Their most recent victim was the tanker *Torrey Canyon* which caused widespread pollution in the winter of 1966/7. The Sevenstones is marked by a lightvessel, the most exposed of any round the British coast, with nothing but her anchor and cable to secure her from driving on to the Cornish coast to leeward. Like all lightvessels, she occupied a station where the construction of a lighthouse is not possible. The violent motion of the hull is very tiring and they are not places for the weak-stomached. Life on lightvessels is fairly monotonous and the lightsmen of the Sevenstones follow the time-honoured routines of seamen everywhere, keep their watch, eat their meals and sleep through their watches below. A man's bunk becomes a haven in heavy weather, a place in which he can jam himself and try to relax and sleep, or to pass the more impossible hours with a book. On watch, there are the absorptions of duty, the rounds of the generators and air compressors, the lookout and the logging of weather – if the weather is fair, routine maintenance. Sometimes as with the grounding of the *Torrey Canyon*, the lightsmen discharge warning signals to vessels heading into danger; some- times the lightvessels themselves are run down by vessels passing too close and making undue allowance for the set of the tide. From time to time during the tour of duty the lightvessel master will order the anchor cable to be inspected while, in the summer, rust-chipping and painting maintain the vessel in between its quadrennial dry-docks. Then it will be taken in tow by one of the tenders and replaced by a temporary lightvessel. At the end of his month, the lightsman comes ashore, usually by helicopter, but occasionally by tender if bad weather disrupts the aircraft's schedule. At night the swaying optic spins slowly in the murette, its beams stabbing the darkness and catching a reflection from an occasional gull. The gleam on the sea's surface is fragmented and soon dissipates, somehow emphasizing the extreme loneliness of the job.

The same huge oceanic movements that suck and claw at the cliffs of Land's End and toss the Sevenstones like a cork, crash against the remote Isles of Scilly a few miles to the south-west. They are low and deadly, rocks, islets and islands beyond counting, with weird names. The main inhabited islands are St Mary's, St Agnes, St Martin's and Tresco; the smaller ones like Gugh, Annet and Samson are largely devoid of human life. The others are too numerous to mention, scattered over an area of some ten square miles, the tombstones of many ships and hundreds of seamen. The Scillonians have a lingering reputation for wreck- ing and for the looting of wrecks. It is not really surprising that a remote and impoverished population sought to enrich itself like this, for wresting a living by fishing, especially in the winter, is very harsh. Even more understandable was the islanders' desire to evade customs duty. In the late eighteenth and early nineteenth century the Scilly gigs, a species of long, light, pulling boats, made almost epic voyages in search of contraband. Usually meeting French vessels at a mid-ocean rendezvous, they also ventured as far afield as Brittany. Such was the seaworthiness of the gigs and the hardiness of their crews that they were almost impossible to catch. When pursued by Revenue cutters, they inevitably pulled directly into the wind's eye, their long hulls leaping from wave-crest to wave- crest, the oar blades dipping and flashing while the over-canvassed cutters tacked fruitlessly in their wake. Despite their unsavoury reputation for showing false lights and murdering half-drowned sailors, the islanders have also carried out some noteworthy rescues. When the great seven-masted American schooner, the *Thomas W. Lawson* got into difficulties in 1907 off the southern rocks, a member of the St Agnes lifeboat crew boarded her to act as pilot. But the ship drove on to Hellweather Neck and was swept by seas. The gig *Slippen* was close but was unable to prevent fifteen men, including the Scillonian pilot, from being washed to their deaths. The pilot's son, Frederick Hicks, jumped from the gig and gallantly swam to the wreck, succeeding in rescuing the master and engineer. The gigs proved very useful in this work for, being light, they could be carried over the islands and launched from sheltered beaches.

Among the hundreds of wrecks that have occurred on the islands, was the German emigrant ship *Schiller* which ran ashore in 1875 with the loss of about 350 lives. A loss of a different kind was sustained on 10 December 1798. HMS *Colossus* was returning from service in the Mediterranean loaded with a number of art treasures collected by the British ambassador at Naples, Sir William Hamilton, the elderly husband of Nelson's Emma. The ship was in a very poor condition, making a great deal of water and her captain, George Murray, worked her into St Mary's Road to avoid bad weather. Unfortunately the ship dragged her anchor and drove ashore on Samson where she broke up with the loss of Sir William's fine collection.

It is not therefore surprising that early attempts were made to mark the Isles of Scilly with a lighthouse. In the seventeenth century Sir John Clayton recommended one but it was Trinity House itself that built and managed the coal-fired lighthouse built on St Agnes in 1680. It was an early example of an enclosed coal fire, the roof of the tower having a number of wide chimneys to carry off the smoke. The light was about 70 feet from the ground and about 200 above high water, making it a comparatively conspicuous seamark for its time. Whether or not it was painted white, is not known, but this is probable. However, building the lighthouse was one thing; collecting the dues quite another. The collector at Cowes reported he was unable to collect the money as "the most considerable persons have joined in a club to obstructing of the collection for Scilly". Another problem was that the light thrown out by the coal fire penetrated the moist air of thick weather very feebly. A coal light remained in service until 1790 when the Elder Brethren returned from a voyage to France where they had observed an improved design of Argand's lamp and, enlarging it, fitted the first revolving light to a British lighthouse at St Agnes. This was further improved in 1806 at the enormous cost of £5,000 when a new optic and revolving engine were installed.

However, the wrecks continued, and the only remedy Trinity House could suggest was building a new lighthouse on the most extreme, south-west rock in the archipelago, since the light on St Agnes might not be seen until a ship was already among the outer reefs. The rock selected was known as the Bishop and in 1837 work began under the overall direction of James Walker. The design Walker selected was derived from a lighthouse on the Smalls Reef off Pembrokeshire which, sixty years before, had been constructed of wooden piles, standing on a latticework through which the sea had free access. In this case, Walker decided to build a screw-pile lighthouse of wrought-iron forming an open

The lighthouse at Hartland Point is threatened by the ceaseless erosion of the Atlantic. In the foreground is the wreck of a coaster.

*Two dramatic sunsets off Round Island, at the northern
extremity of the Isles of Scilly.*

*The lighthouse on Godrevy Island, North Cornwall, was
another tower built by James Walker. Although it is only
a short distance from the shore, the relief of the keepers
was often hampered by the terrible "backwash" effect of
the huge Atlantic swells.*

Trinity House maintain a major depot at Swansea in the
industrial heartland of South Wales. The vessel
responsible for the west coast is based here and there is
also a buoy servicing plant as well as an ancillary service
to the helicopter flights from Swansea Airport.

tower and sank the initial heavy screws into the hard granite. To start with the work went well. By December 1849 the tower waited for the lantern and work was suspended until the following spring. But Walker's deductions were faulty: what worked with resilient timber on the Smalls did not work with rigid iron on the Bishop. On 5 February 1850 a furious gale struck the Isles of Scilly and the following morning the lattice tower had vanished. Undaunted, Walker returned to Smeaton's design and this time selected an area of rock which gave him a diameter of thirty-five feet. Around this he built an iron caisson and pumped the water out, thus allowing the first course of stones to be laid one foot below low water. The work then progressed whenever possible. The men were encamped on an adjacent islet and put under the direction of James Douglass who insisted on sharing their discomforts, teaching them to live "on limpets and puffins' eggs and in the evenings organized concerts to which he contributed solos on the flute". The final tower was almost 120 feet in height and consisted of 2,500 tons of dressed granite, all sent from the mainland, and took seven years to build. It was lit on 1 September 1858. It was this experience which convinced Walker that Smeaton had produced the definitive design and encouraged him to attempt the more difficult task of building the Wolf Rock lighthouse.

In 1881, however, Douglass noted extensive damage and weakness in the structure, especially in its base. He remedied this by completely surrounding the foundation with a massive cylindrical casing of granite bolted to the rock. He then continued this encapsulation upwards, outside the original tower, increasing the weight of the lighthouse by 3,200 tonnes and its height by forty feet. The cost of this was a prodigious £66,000. Since its completion in October 1887, the Bishop Rock has been modernized to keep pace with developments. Today its brilliant electric light is topped by a helipad and the keepers, based at St Mary's, are flown out every month by helicopter.

A small automatic light-beacon at Penninis Head marks the entrance for the mail-ship into St Mary's Sound, but it is mainly of local significance. The northern extremity of the Isles of Scilly is marked by Round Island lighthouse, a short tower on the summit of a precipitously-sided islet between Tresco and St Martin's. The lighthouse was built in 1887 and it proved almost as difficult to hoist the building materials up the steep cliffs as to lay the foundations of sea-washed towers. The island is about 130 feet high but even so, during the severe gales of January 1984, seas smashed the lower doors of the fog-signal house. When first built, the station was fitted with one of three hyper-radial optics, huge structures of glass and bronze designed to maximize the red light this tower exhibits. Red is less effective a light than white and such lenses were necessary to give the required range. Today's half-million candela, electric-powered optic has a range of twenty-four miles and shows a single flash every ten seconds. In fog the powerful siren discharges a blast of compressed air four times every minute.

On a clear night, an observer on Round Island can see the isophase flare of the Longships and, on the mainland, to the north, the group flashing light on

Pendeen Point, situated on the north-west extremity of the Land's End peninsula where the coast trends back eastward towards St Ives. Pendeen is a fairly recent station, built in 1900 and modernized since then. Its white tower and distinctive white dwellings sit on the cliff-top above the sometimes rusty waters of the sea where the waves come into contact with ore deposits in the rocks below.

St Ives is tucked under the lee of the bulge of Land's End, its bay forming an anchorage of sorts in south-westerly gales. But it can turn into a dangerous lee shore if the wind should veer suddenly to the north-west as not infrequently happens. Named after the Irish saint, Ia, who is said to have landed here in the sixth century after a voyage from Ireland in a coracle, the little port was an important centre of the pilchard fishery in the nineteenth century, largely because of the splendid stone pier built in 1770 by our old friend, John Smeaton. Now a centre of tourism, hotels break through the wooded hillside above golden sands that sweep to the north-east, where they choked the channel into Hayle five hundred years ago. The northern end of St Ives Bay is formed by Godrevy Island and a long granite reef called The Stones. Countless ships came to grief upon The Stones and in October 1854 a public outcry followed the loss of the passenger steamer *Nile*. Trinity House reacted by building Godrevy lighthouse to a design by James Walker. It was octagonal in design and made of local rubble, bedded in mortar. The first lights shone out on 1 March 1859, a main light of white showing a red sector over The Stones which run directly out to sea from the island. Today the extremity of the reef is marked by a large buoy. Alterations to the lighting apparatus were carried out in 1939 but nothing improved the island's accessibility. Although only a short distance from the shore, the terrible "backwash" effect caused by the Atlantic swells striking the coast made the relief of the keepers very difficult. Shortly after the Second World War the station was made automatic (running on acetylene) and was left for most of the year to the oyster-catchers, gulls, terns and rock pipits who inhabit its shores. In spring primroses, heather and thrift carpet its short grass while seals and gannets hunt fish off its rocky perimeter. The distant and inaccessible image of Godrevy forms a backdrop to Virginia Woolf's *To the Lighthouse*.

The north coast of Cornwall is a windward coast, that is one upon which the prevailing wind usually blows. With the wind comes the sea and the ceaseless action of the waves pounding constantly against the granite produces a steep-to coast of cliffs, with beaches of sand between the more resistant headlands. Rivers flowing westwards have their estuaries invaded by salt water and their channels choked with sand bars, making entry and departure very difficult. There are few dangers extending far offshore, although islets and rocks may be found within a mile or two of the beach. During the summer months many of these beaches attract surfers but in the winter it is a coast to be avoided by landsmen and seamen alike. There is an old couplet that runs:

From Padstow Bar to Lundy light
Is a sailor's grave by day or night.

The inhabitants of this lonely coast scratched a living from fishing and the looting of wrecks, often blaming the Cornish giants Wrath and Bedruthan, who were reputed to wade out into the sea and snatch ships up! On Watergate Sands, near Newquay, the local population caused a rumpus in 1869 when they did their best to frustrate the attempts of a tug to tow off a ship that had stranded on the sands. The salvage effort was annoying the looters who, since time out of mind, had accepted the proceeds of a wreck as a right. As Killigrew complained, they

A small automatic light-beacon at Penninis Head marks the entrance to St Mary's Sound, on the largest of the Scilly Isles.

regarded it as "God's Grace". During the nineteenth century the pilchard fishery reached its height, bringing a measure of prosperity to a corner of England that remained very primitive. The coming of the railway ensured that the catches were quickly on their way to market and the tiny ports that grew up in the partial shelter of the headlands enjoyed the benefits of commerce for the first time. Newquay was no exception. Sheltering behind Towan Head, its "new" quay was built in 1439 to provide shelter for fishermen. Fishing and smuggling formed its chief "industries", although local ships made trans-Atlantic voyages. In the late 1700s pilchard began to arrive off the Cornish coast in immense shoals and for about 150 years these fish provided a regular source of wealth for the men of

Newquay. A watch for the shoals was kept by the "Huer" who lived in a special house designed for the purpose and which includes a watch tower. When the tell-tale shimmering was sighted the Huer bellowed "Heva! Heva!", alerting the fishermen in the town who ran to their boats and put out to sea with their nets at the ready. The Huer remained at his station, calling out directions to the boats as they closed the shoal, much as a shepherd does to his dog. Some catches were enormous. One landed at Newquay was said to be worth £20,000 and it took two thousand cartloads to carry it away. When the railway came to Newquay in 1875 it not only facilitated the swift removal of fish to market but brought visitors from the east, establishing Newquay as a holiday centre.

Dominating the coast north of Newquay is Trevose Head, with its white lighthouse set into the sloping green of the headland. There was a project to build a light in 1809 but nothing came of it until 1847 when the present tower was built of local stone. An oil reflector light was initially installed but the want of a fog signal was felt, for mist and low visibility are usually produced by the warm moist winds of a south-westerly airstream and the slight rise in the flow of air as it blows inland over the coast is often enough to cool and vaporize it even when it is comparatively clear offshore. Despite protests, it was not until a new optic was installed in 1882 that a fog signal was fitted. The delay was almost over-compensated, for a monstrous square trumpetted horn, 36 feet long, 2 feet deep and 18 feet wide was constructed on the hillside. It was known as "Lord Rayleigh's trumpet" after its inventor, Lord Rayleigh being then the Scientific Adviser to Trinity House. This huge device was driven by compressed air held in large "bottles" at the lighthouse. Off Trevose Head lie the Quies, a little group of islets, the Gulland Rock, Newland and the Mouls, strung across the estuary of the River Camel and barring the entrance to Padstow. Running into the sea between Stepper Point (on which there is a tall white daymark) and Pentire Point, the Camel has to force its way out as the sea attempts to choke its path with sand. In this Padstow is typical of rivers meeting the sea on a weather coast and the resultant bar is aptly and chillingly called Doom Bar. Two more fishing villages nestle beyond Pentire Point and the Mouls, Port Quin and Port Isaac, but the land soon swings northward again, rising towards Tintagel Head.

Nothing more substantial than Tennyson's imagination links Tintagel with King Arthur, but the dramatic meeting of cliffs and ocean, the rocks and caves, even the twelfth-century ruins create a convincing atmosphere, illusory though it is. A great number of remote headlands in Cornwall and west Wales bear the marks of iron age fortification, with ramparts and ditches dug across the isthmus of each promontory. Whoever, or whatever King Arthur was, is immaterial, but it is almost certain that Tintagel was originally fortified like this. Such a primitive defensive position was defended by the sea on three sides and the warriors needed only to man the landward-facing rampart to preserve their families and livestock. The ruins that remain at Tintagel are those of the great hall, built by Reginald, Earl of Cornwall in 1145. Henry III's brother Richard added landward walls connected to the "island" by a drawbridge, thus strengthening the original inner ward.

The cliffs continue north of Tintagel, rising to the Cambeak six miles to the north. Here they reach 730 feet above mean sea level, forming a dramatic and wild scene during an onshore gale. The hard core of more resistant rock that forms the pointed Cambeak itself falls away and a mile or so further north the expanse of Widemouth Sand covers the British end of the White House to Downing Street hotline. In an age of less apocalyptic preoccupations Bude was noted for its exports of lime-enriched sand, much used for manure. The harbour entrance is narrow and tricky, but the port existed for many years, chiefly because of the canal that connected it with Launceston inland. The canal rises 350 feet in its six miles of length and contains only one lock. The rest of the lift was achieved by using wooden tub-boats. These ran up a simple wooden railway powered by a system of counter-weights which drew the tub-boats along. An example of one of these, half-boat, half-truck, is preserved at the maritime museum at Exeter.

Deeply incised cliffs continue north beyond Bude, culminating in Higher Sharpnose Point. Atop the point, the dish aerials of the satellite tracking station gleam in sunlight, highly conspicuous from a considerable distance at sea. Behind the headland nestles Morwenstow, named for the patron of its parish church, St Morwenna. In 1834 Robert Stephen Hawker became its parish priest. In an age when the clergy were eager to be considered gentry, Hawker adopted the dress of a fisherman and harangued his congregation on the evils of wrecking and the looting of wrecks. Something of an eccentric, he once confounded his superstitious parishioners by dressing himself up as a mermaid and appeared on a rock combing his "hair". After a suitably wide-eyed and gullible crowd had assembled, pointing the "mermaid" out knowingly to their friends, Hawker rose and, standing on his "tail", gave them a deafening rendition of "God Save the Queen". Among Hawker's talents was that of poet, his *The Quest of the Sangraal, Chant the First* of 1864 being considered his best work. He was better known, however, for his *Cornish Ballads* of 1869 among which *The Song of the Western Men* achieved popularity after being set to music. It contained the famous lines written in 1688 when Bishop Trelawney was in the Tower of London during the troubles caused by King James II's Roman Catholicism:

> *And have they fixed the where and when?*
> *And shall Trelawney die?*
> *Here's twenty thousand Cornishmen*
> *Will know the reason why!*

Ironically Hawker was received into the Roman Catholic church on his deathbed, in August 1875.

Cliffs run on to the north of Morwenstow and the inhospitable nature of this coast was so feared by mariners that as early as the sixteenth century Raleigh,

Drake and Hawkins clubbed together to finance the little breakwater known as Hartland Quay. It is no more than a beckoning finger of rocky welcome but it must have been a boon to exhausted seamen in days when ships were small enough to tuck themselves behind it. During heavy weather it can have been of little value though, for the action of the sea on the tall carboniferous cliffs of Hartland Point is tremendous. The lost river valley of Wargery Water gives a clear illustration of its strength. This river runs northwards, parallel to the coast, emptying itself into Barnstaple Bay, but the west side of its valley has disappeared, consumed by the sea. Between Bude and Hartland Point the folding of the rock strata is evidence of a titanic struggle. These natural forces continue to act upon the cliffs and the sea has been estimated to pound Hartland's cliffs at a pressure of four tons per square foot. Its destructive power presented problems to Trinity House in preserving the lighthouse at Hartland Point which was built in 1874. Set below the normal level of the cloud base, it seems to crouch hunchbacked below the rising land behind it, half fearful of the next depression and its westerly gales. Soon after its building, the lighthouse was threatened by undermining and tons of boulders were broken away from behind the tower and tipped beneath the cliffs. They were quickly washed away and, after successive experiments of a like nature had been made, a sea wall was built in 1925. The Romans called Hartland Point the Promontory of Hercules, because it seemed to defy the elements so heroically. Despite the erosion that we know to be taking place ceaselessly, this is an enduring image. Hartland Point may submit eventually to the ceaseless onslaught of the mighty Atlantic, but it will be a moment in time far beyond the imagination of the present.

CHAPTER EIGHT

THE TIDE TRIUMPHANT

Lundy South.

From Hartland Point in the south to St Ann's Head on the Pembroke coast to the north, the Bristol Channel is some forty-five miles across. It is an ever-narrowing funnel, open to the west and subject to very high spring tides at its eastern end. The spring range at Avonmouth is the second greatest in the world, surpassed only by the height of tide in the Bay of Fundy, Nova Scotia. Here the sea has invaded the land on a massive scale, exploiting the River Severn as it makes its way into the Atlantic, rushing right into the estuary, often rising eighteen feet in an hour and a half to form the famous Severn bore. This is a wave of water of a different height from the river itself, derived from a Scandinavian word for billow. It is sometimes called an "eagre".

The sea's first incursion begins behind Hartland Point where the great cliffs of Gallantry Bower (which fall to the steep hillside village of Clovelly) give way to the low flats surrounding the combined estuaries of the Rivers Taw and Torridge. A great sweep of sand fronts the dunes as the two rivers struggle out through the piled-up banks, its channel navigable only at high-water and then liable to shifting. The Taw and Torridge meet off Instow, near the ancient shipbuilding town of Appledore. A fishing village in Saxon times, Appledore was granted status as a freeport by Queen Elizabeth I for its part in the defeat of the Spanish Armada. Like neighbouring Barnstaple and Bideford, Appledore provided ships and men for the impromptu fleet collected by Lord Howard of Effingham and Drake in 1588 to harry the great invasion fleet as it made its ponderous way up Channel. The two estuaries are bedevilled by swiftly flowing tidal streams which carve their way through the sand and, at low water, recede to provide miles of feeding ground for waders and sea ducks, especially migrant eiders. It was here that Henry Williamson's *Tarka the Otter* learned about the vastness of the ocean. As well as shifting, the approach channel is often made hazardous by heavy swells which roll steeply up the shallowing bed of Barnstaple Bay to break on the bar with a loud roar.

The rock strata of north Devon run parallel to the coast, so at Baggy Point and Morte Point, before the coast swings east, they form folds of hard rock, producing the two points and the intervening bays of Croyde and Mortehoe. Baggy Point was the last resting place of the smack *Ceres*, for many years the oldest craft listed in Lloyd's Register. Built in 1811, she was 125 years old at the time of her grounding and loss in 1936. Off-lying rocks exist at both points, the

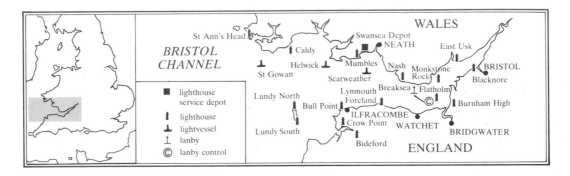

Morte Stone, off Morte Point, being a particular danger as the tide races round the corner, in and out of the Bristol Channel, with a steady ferocity. Both rocks are marked by buoys. As the coast turns east, a clutch of rocks chokes Rockham Bay, closed on its far side by Bull Point. The lighthouse here throws a constant red light over the Morte Stone.

Bull Point lighthouse was built in 1879 and, like so many stations established at this time, for many years was notable only for quiet service to the seafaring community. But in September 1972 a dramatic event took place. After preliminary cracks had opened up on the 18th, during the early hours of Sunday, 24 September, fifty feet of the cliff fell away, taking with it part of the lighthouse generator engine-room and fog-signal installation. The exposed strata on Bull Point is of shale, a rock much affected by erosion, split as it is by tiny seams, exploited by the sea. The loss of the engine-room put the light out of use and later that day the tender arrived from Swansea with a hurriedly prepared buoy which was laid to mark the extremity of the rock-fall and provide a much diminished but recognizable substitute for the lighthouse. The lighthouse itself was replaced a few days later by borrowing one of the old Instow leading lights. This was a lattice tower, built originally for use in the Red Sea, which had been taken into service as the front leading light at Instow. Replaced in due course, it had then been given to the nature reserve at Braunton Burrows for use as an elevated bird-watching hide. The trustees of the reserve generously responded to Trinity House's appeal and the lighthouse optic was hurriedly rigged up on top of this elderly tower. The problem of the lost fog-signal was less easily solved. The only moveable fog-signal available was that on board the west-coast spare lightvessel held in readiness at Swansea. Trinity House therefore decided to take the unusual step of

*The lighthouse at Bull Point was built in 1974 to replace
one destroyed by a dramatic rock fall in September 1972.*

The old lighthouse tower on Lundy Island can still be seen (above), but it was replaced in 1897 by two new towers, one at the south end of the island (below) and an unmanned one at the north.

mooring a lightvessel off the point for the purpose of providing a fog signal alone. Meanwhile, design of a new lighthouse was quickly put in hand, utilizing much of the equipment already at the station, but modifying it to run by itself. Work was carried out in 1974 and completed at a cost of £71,000. In order to build the new tower on land unlikely to slip during the foreseeable future, a plot had to be specially purchased from the National Trust.

The present lighthouse runs constantly, the two-panel optic being driven by a gearless electric motor and showing three flashes of white light every ten seconds. The fog signal operates automatically, coming on when water vapour in the air reaches a certain percentage. The fog signal generates four blasts every minute at 120 decibels. The three trumpets are driven by compressed air which is stored in massive accumulators at the base of the tower. Its emitters are an integral part of the tower wall, made of a mixture of cement to which cinders have been added to retain a certain resonant elasticity. On completion of the building, the old tower was demolished, the temporary light returned to Braunton Burrows, and the lightvessel towed away. The station was reduced to "keeper and wife" status, the single keeper working normal hours to carry out routine checks but with his bungalow linked to an alarm system.

From Bull Point to Porlock the coast is formed from the northern extremity of Exmoor, a swift declivity of red and grey rock, dropping almost sheer to the sea and in places thick with vegetation. Here and there a small combe shelters a meadow and attractive houses nestle in clefts; waterfalls spill over the cliff-edge and each cove is as lovely in summer as it is terrible in a winter gale. Small towns such as Ilfracombe and Lynmouth, centres of the tourist trade, huddle in river valleys between the rocky promontories that overlook the hurrying and victorious tide as it floods eastwards towards Bristol and Avonmouth. The cliffs are seamed with fissures and caves, ideal for smugglers. At Ilfracombe, one of Thomas à Becket's murderers, De Tracey, is said to have hidden while his servant brought a small vessel round from Barnstaple. He is supposed to have lived in France until the death of King Henry II in 1189 when he returned to Devon to build the church at Mortehoe and become its first priest, an atonement for his terrible crime.

Lynmouth was badly damaged in 1952 after a particularly heavy downpour on the moor above. The flooding freshets burst upon Lynmouth and washed away numerous houses, causing widespread damage. The village has been rebuilt and is once again as charming as when it was discovered by the romantic poets of the early nineteenth century (Wordsworth, Coleridge and Shelley all spent some time at Lynmouth in the early 1800s), although the coast is better remembered today as the scene of *Lorna Doone*, written by Richard Doddridge Blackmore in 1869. Some idea of the forces which folded the rock layers can be seen in the western face of Lynmouth Foreland. These are hog's back cliffs, in which the dip and scarp slopes are steep, resulting in long, narrow ridges. The gentler grassy slopes of the headlands east and west of the Foreland are absent here and the gradient is dangerously steep and scree-covered.

This situation compelled the builders of the lighthouse in 1900 to construct it a mere two hundred feet above mean sea level, to avoid the heavy orographic cloud which frequently shrouds the Foreland's summit. The lighthouse is therefore cut into the slope, a huge sixty-foot-high buttressed retaining wall forming the southern boundary of the compound. The keepers' dwellings are above the level of the lighthouse itself. The present electric light generates one million candelas and has a character of four white flashes every fifteen seconds. Despite the thick weather that frequently engulfs this area, the original building did not incorporate a fog signal which was added later. Against the dark, grey-green of the beetling Foreland, the white tower and its white retaining wall can be seen twenty miles away in clear weather.

Astride the tidal invasion round Bull Point and some fifteen miles westward lies Lundy Island. Deriving from the Norse word for puffin, regrettably few of these charming little "sea-parrots" are seen today on, or near the island. Nevertheless it is the nesting place for many other species. Kittiwakes, razorbills and guillemots form the largest section of the breeding population, vying with each other for tiny ledge sites on Lundy's magnificent brown cliffs. Herring gulls, both species of black-backed gulls, gannets, jackdaws and the massive wedge-tailed ravens whose spectacular aerobatic courtship displays may be seen in the spring, are all also easily spotted around the island. So, too, are cormorants and shags, wagtails, wheatears, rock pipits and finches. The grassy moorland provides a habitat for these and other passerine birds, many on migration. The inhabitants keep Soay sheep and wild goats. The narrow island is almost unapproachable upon its steep, rock-littered western side. Trinity House once maintained a fog-signal station on this coast, about half-way down the cliff. It was fitted with a pair of muzzle-loading cannon which were fired at regular intervals in fog or thick weather. The embrasures and powder store may still be seen. This fog signal station was attached to the original lighthouse, built on the summit of the island.

Lundy is the remains of a shale-covered granite mountain. Most of the shale has long since disappeared, but some remains at the south bay where it forms an eroding saddle, linking the granite mass of the main island with the outcrops on which the present south lighthouse is built. There is a fine anchorage at Lundy Road in south-west and north-west gales which has been dominated by Marisco Castle since about 1240. The castle was built by a certain Robert de·Marisco who claimed title from a grant of land made by Henry III. Marisco started a tradition of piracy, wrecking and pillaging which formed the main occupation of the island's tiny and desperate population for many years. The number of inhabitants reached its apogee during the last decade of the nineteenth century under the ownership of the Heaven family. It was during this period that St Helen's church with its conspicuous square tower was built.

The island has become the graveyard for hundreds of ships and some have given their names to features on Lundy's coast. In 1797 the *Jenny* of Bristol ran into a little cove on the west side. She carried a cargo of ivory and gold dust, long since washed out of her pulverized hull, leaving only her name at Jenny Cove as a reminder of her fate. Caught in the anchorage of Lundy Road by a veering wind, the *Hannah Moore* drove from her anchors and grounded on Rat Island (so named for being the last home of the once common Black Rat) in January 1866. A gallant rescue attempt was made by two islanders, but the ship soon began to break up. Six of her crew got on to rocks and, after five attempts, they were rescued. The others all perished. In February 1892 the French ship *Tunisie* ran aground on the rocks close to the south lighthouse. John McCarthy, the principal keeper, organized rocket line-throwing apparatus and succeeded in rigging up an extempore breeches-buoy using an old coal sack. For this McCarthy, his assistant keepers and some itinerant labourers were awarded fifteen shillings (75p) each by the RNLI for their "gallant and successful exertions in rescuing the crew of 21 persons" from the *Tunisie*. The Board of Trade also made an award of three pounds to each man; two Elder Brethren travelled to Lundy to make the presentation.

Despite all the sophistication of modern aids to navigation, vessels are still wrecked on Lundy. The most recent was the West German coaster *Kaaksburg*, which ran aground on the east side below Tibbett's Point in November 1980. Although this is on the island's lee side, the ship rapidly broke her back and disintegrated. But the most famous and most embarrassing twentieth-century wreck was that of HMS *Montagu*, a first-class battleship which cost the British tax-payer the then enormous sum of one million pounds. She was only five years old in May 1906 when she was engaged in secret wireless tests off the north coast of Cornwall. In dense fog, her navigating staff thought they were off Hartland Point when she struck rocks off the south-west corner of the island, close to Shutter Point. No lives were lost and other units of the Channel Fleet, the *Montagu*'s sister ships *Duncan*, *Exmouth*, *Albemarle* and *Cornwallis*, arrived to offer assistance. But the *Montagu* was stuck fast and repeated efforts to refloat her met with ignominious failure. Apart from the scandal because a capital ship of the Royal Navy was involved, this incident was not particularly remarkable before the invention of radar. What made the wreck of HMS *Montagu* memorable was the salvage operation that followed, directed from the Liverpool salvage ships *Linnet* and *Ranger*. After it was discovered that she could not be refloated, the decision was made to take out of her all her stores and her enormously heavy guns, the barrels of which each weighed several tons. Aerial runways and cat-walks were rigged from the cliff, high above, and a small army of labourers was encamped on the island. Frequently hampered by the heavy swells that break on Shutter Point, the removal of so much equipment must rate as a considerable achievement, even though the ship herself was lost. The irony was that the *Montagu* ran aground shortly after Trinity House had been to considerable expense to improve the navigational aids on Lundy after centuries of complaints.

In 1786 a group of Bristol merchants had obtained a patent for a lighthouse on the island and began its construction in the next year. It was never completed and the matter lapsed until Trinity House proposed building one in 1819. Work was completed in 1822 and a splendid building was erected on Beacon Hill, a high point on the western side of the island. Unfortunately the site chosen was frequently shrouded in cloud and the builders made the mistake of fitting two vertical white lights; the upper revolved, the lower was shown from a window to the west and fixed in character. The upper light revolved with such speed that no discernible eclipse could be seen from seaward and the lights merged. In November 1828 another French vessel, *La Jeune Emma*, on passage from Martinique to Cherbourg and badly out in her reckoning, mistook the Lundy light for that on Ushant. When she struck the island thirteen of the nineteen people on board were lost, one of whom was a niece of the former French Empress Josephine. There was a public outcry about the inefficiency of the lighthouse rather than the poor navigation of the ship's master! To answer its critics, Trinity House temporized and, half-way down the cliff below the lighthouse, built a pair of embrasures and a powder store. Muzzle-loading cannon were installed to be fired in foggy weather as a warning to ships approaching Lundy from the west. The remains of this battery and the original lighthouse may still be seen.

Clearly this was only a partial solution and it was not until a general improvement in all the coastal lighthouses of Cornwall, Devon and West Wales took place that Trinity House improved matters. In 1897 the original single tower was replaced by two lighthouses, one at either end of the island, and both built below the level of the cloud base. On a dark damp night, such as is frequent in the Western Approaches, the beams from these two lights may be seen revolving just below the level of the orographic cloud that lies like a table cloth over Lundy island. Originally these two lights were powered by vaporized paraffin burners intensified by large Fresnel lenses, each over a ton in weight and floating in mercury. So delicately balanced were they that it was possible to turn them by the application of a finger. The mechanical revolving apparatus was clockwork, driven by a weight falling through an iron column down the centre of the tower and wound up every half an hour. Both lights had compressed air fog signals. Fuel was brought from Swansea by lighthouse tender and hoisted ashore in barrels where it was tipped into the station's tanks by hand.

Today only the southern light is fully manned and the performance of the north light is monitored from it, routine visits being made periodically by a keeper from Lundy South. Fuelling is carried out at both stations by helicopter and tender in a combined operation now common to all remote lighthouses, whether manned or automated. Gas, oil and fresh water are flown in, underslung beneath the helicopter which airlifts neoprene tanks from the flight deck of the ship. If needed, a working party of an officer and seamen is first flown in to attend to the pumps and pipework. This highly co-ordinated task employs the services of a Bolkow 105D helicopter of Bond Helicopters Ltd, two of which are on permanent charter to Trinity House and are painted in the Corporation's livery. This small but highly adaptable and powerful aircraft is capable of underslinging up to 400 kilos on short flights and these loads are not necessarily confined to fuel and water but may consist of machinery, other stores, spare parts, building materials and so forth. Operating with a helicopter enables the tender to carry out the refuelling of lighthouses in far worse weather and sea conditions than was the case when all stores had to be transferred to ship's boats and sent into the rock-strewn landings for delivery.

Lundy Island is a detached remnant of a granite mass which also forms Exmoor, beyond which the land falls away, shallow water extends offshore and in the tiny ports of Minehead and Watchet, craft must take the ground at low water. At Hinkley Point a nuclear power station rears its unlovely profile against the eastern horizon. Behind it the flat fens of the Somerset levels stretch away like some surprising western evocation of the Cambridge fens. Here, history alleges, King Alfred burnt a cottager's miserable oat cakes, while at Glastonbury the Arthurian legend lingers on. In her magnificent and highly plausible reconstruction of the story of Arthur, *Sword at Sunset*, Rosemary Sutcliff conceives the death of the king here, among the marshes and the apple orchards of Somerset. The historical facts relating to the end of the Duke of Monmouth's brief rebellion of 1685 among the reeds of Sedgemoor are more certain. Essentially a peasant rising of poor puritans against the Catholicism of James II, Monmouth found little support elsewhere. The labourers, yeomen, miners and shopkeepers of Somerset and Devon who flocked to the standard of Charles II's bastard did so in support of their religion. Monmouth's uncle, King James II, already under attack by the Commons for his dogged adherence to Roman Catholicism and a covert alliance with France, sent the Guards and some troops recently returned from service in Tangier. Monmouth crossed his own Rubicon when he declared himself the rightful king. Falling back from Bristol, he decided on a surprise attack on the royal army in its camp near Bridgwater. The surprise miscarried and the professional soldiers cut the unfortunate rebels to pieces. Victory was not tempered by magnanimity. After the battle Judge Jeffreys was sent down and held a circuit of "Bloody Assizes". The roadsides of Wessex were lined with the bodies of three hundred and fifty dissenters, eight hundred were sold into slavery in the West Indies (a fact Rafael Sabatini used in his swash-buckling novel *Captain Blood*) and numerous people, including women, were whipped and imprisoned. The cruelty which followed the rebel defeat even affected John Churchill (later the great Duke of Marlbrough) whose energy had largely carried the day at Sedgemoor in the king's name. "This marble", he said as he struck an overmantel on which he was leaning, "is not harder than the king's heart."

Many of the dykes that ran red with the blood of Monmouth's loyal and misguided troops drain into the River Parrett which meanders through this flat landscape past Burnham-on-Sea and pushes out through vast mudflats to the open sea. Stert Flats and Berrow Flats form a huge feeding ground for waders and ducks. Again the prevailing winds and strong tides combine to make the Parrett's path to the sea a difficult one. The channel moves frequently and its navigation is difficult. As early as 1815 Trinity House established a pair of leading lights at Burnham-on-Sea, but inexplicably they turned their management over to a lessee, the Rev. David Davies who was ambitious to make the town into a spa. The light was acquired after the 1836 Act and today consists of a single automatic beacon with differing sector colours to assist vessels to hold the deep water of the channel. These can be altered more easily than moving a front light which was situated on the flats. The old front light is still there, a red and white wooden structure on stilts.

A little upstream of Burnham stands Bridgwater, home of Robert Blake who became the MP for the town in 1640. On the outbreak of the Civil War he declared for Parliament and achieved considerable military success. After the execution of Charles I, Blake was one of three army officers nominated "Generals-at-Sea", the Parliamentary equivalent of admiral. He destroyed the Royalist fleet off Cartagena in November 1650, and in May of the following year captured the Isles of Scilly for Parliament. In 1652 war broke out with the Dutch and Blake gained two victories, off Dover and the Kentish Knock, but was badly mauled by Van Tromp off Dungeness on 30 November 1652. Three further battles were fought with the Dutch in which Blake gained the upper hand, despite stiff opposition. He died at sea in 1657 within sight of Plymouth, weakened by scurvy and suffering from dropsy. Buried in Westminster Abbey, Charles II ordered his body to be exhumed at the Restoration when it was reinterred in St Margaret's next door. Clarendon, the Royalist historian and contemporary of Blake's, said of him "He was the first man to bring ships to contemn *[sic]* castles on the shore, which had ever been thought very formidable." Dr Johnson wrote of Robert Blake, "Nor has any writer dared to deny him the praise on intrepidity, honesty, contempt of wealth, and love of his country."

Beyond Berrow Flats a high ridge of hard carboniferous limestone is prominent, one of three parallel ridges interspersed with low land fringed by extensive sands. Brean Down was fortified by Palmerston in 1867. The fort, one of a chain across the Bristol Channel, was located low on the extremity of the headland and was garrisoned until 1900 by about fifty men of the Royal Garrison Artillery. Armed with huge and clumsy 8-inch muzzle-loading Armstrong rifled guns, the fort was abandoned after the magazine exploded. Off Weston-super-mare comparatively shallow water extends seaward across to the island of Steepholm. The limestone ridge extends right across the Bristol Channel via the neighbouring island of Flatholm, to the Welsh coast at Lavernock Point. Extensive sandbanks are cut by deep channels through which the Avon, Severn, Wye and Usk drain to the sea. All are buoyed by Trinity House and lead to the ports of Bristol, Avonmouth, Sharpness, Newport and Cardiff.

The rise of Bristol as a major port began in the last years of the fifteenth century. Originally a Saxon port, it was not until John Cabot discovered New-foundland (June 1497) and opened English eyes to the possibilities of acquiring colonies in the New World that Bristol's real prosperity began. Only 120 miles west of London, it was immediately accessible to the Atlantic without the tedious necessity of beating down Channel. Bristol had the additional advantage that if the winds were not favourable, then ships could "tide-down" the Avon to the sea, anchoring when the tide was foul. It was a lengthy and dangerous business but where money and profit beckon men are not slow to take up the challenge. The shallowness of the Avon led eventually to the establishment of a system of docks nearer the sea at Avonmouth. With Newport, Cardiff and Barry, Avonmouth formed a quartet of important ports during the height of Britain's commercial prosperity, but they have all been badly hit by recession. It is at Avonmouth that British tides reach their greatest range, some 12.3 metres at springs. With this phenomenal action the sea exacts its tribute; every ebb tide drags out of the Usk, the Taff, the Wye, the Avon and the mighty Severn itself a brown sediment of eroded soil, the trunks of undermined trees, in short the detritus of a rich and provident hinterland.

Cardiff's fortunes as a port have declined since the cessation of coal exporting from its once busy tips. Dominated by the high land at Penarth, the coast swings west at Lavernock Point. Rocky spits jut seawards, beset by cross tides, making navigation tricky.

The island of Steepholm, as its name implies, is high and isolated and a contrast with its lower neighbour, Flatholm. It has been fortified at different times but is now a nature reserve, being the only British home of the wild peony, a Mediterranean flower introduced by monks in the Middle Ages.

A light had been demanded on the island of Flatholm as early as 1733 by the Merchant Venturers of Bristol, but no formal petition was made to the Crown. An abortive attempt was made to get backing for the light but it failed. In 1736, however, a military transport was wrecked on the island with the loss of many men and war materials. This spurred official interest, a lease was hurriedly drawn up, the tower built and a light shown on 1 December 1737. The costs of running the lighthouse proved too much for the original lessee and he went bankrupt, surrendering the interest to one Caleb Dickenson, who wisely accepted full responsibility not only for the light but for the collection of dues. On 22 December 1790 bad weather occurred and Flatholm was struck by lightning. "We expected every moment to be our last. At three o'clock on the morning of the 23rd the tower was struck by lightning. The man attending the fire was knocked down and narrowly escaped falling through the stairway. The iron fire grate was smashed to pieces and the top of the tower was considerably damaged." A temporary fire was lit in front of the lighthouse whilst a new grate was installed but this efficiency did not last and complaints about the quality of the light were received at Trinity House. It was about this time that experiments were carried out to introduce a matrix of gas jets in the shape of an anchor on Flatholm; nothing seems to have come of this rather fanciful idea, however, and in 1819 Trinity House made an arrangement with Caleb's successor, William Dickenson, which amounted to an assumption of responsibility. The tower was enlarged and raised, the light being altered to a fixed white argand apparatus which was shown from 7 September 1820. Two years later an Act of Parliament enabled Trinity House to buy out Dickenson's remaining financial interest. Further improvements were made in 1825 when the lantern was raised a second time and in 1867 a new lantern was fitted which remained in use for a century, till the station was converted to electric power in 1969. The method of lighting the 1867 optic varied as time passed. It became an occulting light in 1881, having a copper cowl lowered by a clockwork mechanism to eclipse the light. In 1904 and 1923 various differing burner units were put in to keep pace with the alterations and improvements being developed with paraffin vapour burners. In 1908 a powerful fog signal was added, huge, air-operated trumpets being located to point up and down the main channel that runs between Flatholm and Steepholm. The lighthouse became a "rock" station in 1929, the keepers' wives and children being sent ashore and the keepers moving to new accommodation built, inexplicably, adjacent to the fog signal trumpets!

Flatholm is reputedly haunted. The spectre, a "white-lady", is variously said to have been a victim of cholera (for which the island had an isolation hospital) or the wife of one of the keepers. The founding of Woodspring Priory near Brean Down by William de Courtenay, grandson of one of the assassins of Thomas à Becket, has given rise to the legend that the island contains the unhallowed grave of another of Thomas à Becket's murderers. Like Brean Down, the island was heavily fortified by Lord Palmerston. There is a massive water catchment area with an underground reservoir and several of the old muzzle-loading Armstrong guns are still in existence. Most of the original bastions and barracks were revived in the Second World War. Today they are overrun by nettles, brambles and rabbit warrens.In the spring the island is dotted white with the brooding of herring gulls, large and predatory birds who can be very determined in defence of their nests.

West of Barry, the coast becomes bleaker. The silted harbour of Aberthaw is now dominated by a power station and cement works, but cliffs swiftly rise as the coast runs westward. Cliffs and foreshore are composed of limestone, heavily striated horizontally by clay beds of Liassic age. The beach towards Nash Point is of tumbled boulders and there are caves in this extraordinary rock. These flat-etched cliffs culminate at Nash Point and although the coast swings north, the limestone beds continue west, covered by sand to form one of the many dangerous shoals in the area. Because of its extreme length (some seven miles), the Nash Sand was originally marked by a pair of lighthouses whose transit led the mariner clear to the south of the shoal. Built in 1832 by James Walker, they followed the loss of the passenger steamer *Frolic* which emphasized the need for lights on Nash Point. Originally fitted with fixed lights, the lower light was abandoned somewhere about the turn of the century and the high light left with an occulting light. Recent electrification of the higher tower was combined with conversion to a flashing character but both towers are still to be seen. Nash Point has an unremarkable history. Only one episode stands out: in 1977 it was found that due to the immoderate use of chemical fertilizers, insecticides and weedkillers, the compound at the lighthouse represented all that was left of typical meadowland in the Vale of Glamorgan, including the only example of *Cirsium Tuberosum*, the Tuberous Thistle, now extant in the area.

Nash Point is the eastern end of the great bight of Swansea Bay which lies like a bass-clef tipped at forty-five degrees. Much strewn by sandbanks, sur-

The lighthouse at Nash Point, fifteen miles west of Cardiff, is encircled by wild cliffs and lonely bays.

rounded by the dark, rounded hills of Wales, its littoral is strewn with a litter of chimneys, cracking towers, flares, cooling towers and all the industrial parapher-nalia of Port Talbot's steel and chemical works, the distant refinery at Llandarcy and the industrial mish-mash of Swansea. At night the eastern side of the bay has a hellish look, contrasting with the fairy-like strings of road and house lights that are strung out round the western shore of the bay to the Mumbles Head. At Sker Point, a few miles south of the new harbour at Port Talbot, there occurred one of the worst lifeboat disasters of this century. In 1947 the Mumbles lifeboat went to the assistance of the steamship *Samtampa*. In appalling weather the lifeboat closed the wreck but was then overwhelmed by the violence of the seas breaking over the Sker Rocks and was lost with all hands.

For the most part Swansea Bay is shallow and approachable only above half-tide and rising. Trinity House maintains a major depot at Swansea, serving the vessel responsible for the west coast, the offshore maintenance of the fabric of lighthouses, operating a buoy servicing plant and an ancillary service to the helicopter flights made from Swansea Airport. The bay is closed by the Mumbles Head and the off-lying shoal of the Mixon. The light on the Mumbles was built in 1793 by a certain William Jernegan and the Harbour Trustees at Swansea. It passed eventually to the management of the British Transport Docks Board and,

The lighthouse on the Mumbles guides ships into
Swansea Bay.

in 1975, to Trinity House. It is situated within an eighteenth-century fort built on the islet forming the headland and uses a wind generator to provide supplementary power.

From the Mumbles westward, the southern flank of the Gower Peninsula is a magnificent stretch of great headlands cut into by re-entrants that form superb bays with fine stretches of sandy beach. The Gower is what remains of an eroded mountain and consists largely of carboniferous limestone, millstone grit and old red sandstone. Faults at right angles to the coast have been invaded by the sea to form the smaller bays, while synclines, or downward dips of the strata, form the larger sweeps of Oxwich and Porth Eynon Bays. The red sandstone reaches a prominent height in the west, the only point at which it touches the sea, rising in Harding's Down above the long white beach of Rhossilli Bay. The limestone runs further west, beneath the Helwick Sand and in the hump-backed feature of the Worm's Head. This is unmarked by a lighthouse as it lies behind the long spit of the Helwick Sand, itself marked by a lightvessel.

Beyond the Worm's Head, Carmarthen Bay opens up to reveal the ultimate victory of the ocean. Once the Gower and Tenby peninsulas, including Caldey Island, were joined together and themselves united with the Vale of Glamorgan. The north side of the Gower dips away to salt marsh and the estuary of the Loughor, possessing sandbanks as mysterious as those of the Dee or the Wash, full of seabirds and waders. Behind the flood-plain of the Loughor, the hills press closer, squeezing the confluence of the Tywi and Taf at Ferryside. Beyond the junction of the two rivers is Laugharne, best known for its connections with Dylan Thomas who wrote *Under Milk Wood* in a boat-shed on its "mussel-pooled and herring-priested" foreshore.

The hills encroach increasingly upon the shoreline, backing the white beaches of Pendine used in the 1920s for the British land speed record attempts. They are now considered far too short for such things but Sir Malcom Campbell achieved fame upon them and Parry Thomas met his death at the wheel of his car "Babs" while making such an attempt. The car spent forty years in the sand until it was disinterred recently, to be preserved at Capel Curig. Hard rock reappears at Saundersfoot and Tenby. Sandersfoot originally exported anthracite but, like its larger neighbour Tenby, it is now largely a holiday centre. Tenby, or "Denbigh of the fish" is a collection of brightly coloured Georgian and Regency terraces when seen from the sea, so that one is apt to forget the town grew up round the castle on its headland. In 1644 the garrison of Royalists was besieged and bombarded from the land and sea, finally capitulating to the Roundheads. The town became a fashionable watering place during the Napoleonic War and St Catherine's Isle attracted the notice of Palmerston's military engineers during the Second French Empire. It is claimed that the man who introduced algebra to Britain, the Tudor mathematician Robert Recorde, was born at Tenby, a fact that many may view with a jaundiced eye.

A murderous limestone reef breaks the surface of the sea at low water off Tenby. The Woolhouse Rocks were once marked by a beacon, but this was replaced by a buoy in the 1860s. The limestone beds run southward from the land where they merge with the old red sandstone of Caldey Island. Caldey is not very high, a torn-off remnant of rich arable farmland, reminiscent of the Vale of Glamorgan and now worked by the monks of Caldey Abbey. The cliffs and rock formations, particularly their red, striated appearance are arresting, and the soil is said to be very fertile. The present monks are Cistercians, a comparatively modern foundation of this ancient order and one which has replaced the original Benedictines who came to Caldey in the twelfth century. There has been a lighthouse on the summit of the island since 1829 and it is now acetylene-powered, unmanned and automatic. The western end of the island is fantastically fissured limestone with stacks standing offshore. The neighbouring islet of St Margaret's is topped by old ruins and lies opposite Giltar Point across Caldey Sound. Giltar Point is also heavily cracked and split, and marks the edge of the Pembrokeshire coast which trends west and then abruptly south to Stackpole Head and St Govan's Head. A fresh outcrop of red sandstone exists at Great Castle Head (one of several headlands so named in this locality), but for the most part this coast is a grey-brown limestone which the sea has slowly eroded, eating out the weaker veins, exploding the inner strata to form caves and stacks. At St Govan's Head a small chapel nestles in a tiny cove. Some say that St Govan was the Arthurian knight Sir Gawain and scholars agree that whatever transformations the legends have gone through, Gawain is one of the original companions of the king. The early English tradition says of him that he was "gay, gratious *[sic]* and gude". Gawain was cousin to Arthur on his mother's side, reputedly the son of King Loth of Orkney. In early versions of the legends he appears to be the pre-eminent figure and Excalibur was his, not Arthur's, sword. He is thought to have much in common with the Irish hero Cuchullin from whom some of the plot in *Sir Gawain and the Green Knight* was poached. It is asserted that Gawain enjoyed the favours of a fairy lady and knew of the existence of an "Isle of Maidens". A local story connects St Margaret's Isle with a nunnery but Gawain seems to pre-date the Christian tradition and the hermit who built the little stone chapel has almost certainly nothing to do with him.

In one of the tiny indentations along the coast between St Govan's Head and Linney Head, stands the Elegug Stacks. Named from the Welsh for guillemot (*heligog*), these twin rock towers are the breeding place of guillemots, razorbills, fulmars and kittiwakes. Linney Head is a great buttress of rock, broken offshore into a number of residual and dangerous fragments.

Five and a half miles away, St Ann's lighthouse is built upon cliffs of a brilliant deep red hue and marks the entrance to Milford Haven. The whole of Milford Haven is formed out of the flooded valley of the River Cleddau, the sea having flung itself against the old red sandstone, revealing its distinctive colour. Milford Haven is one of Britain's great tanker ports, specially provided by its own authority with extensive aids to navigation, although Trinity House maintain the buoyage. Despite the depth of the natural ria, extensive rock-blasting was done in the late 1960s to accommodate the deep draughts of large tankers. The oldest town on the shores of the Haven is Pembroke, birthplace of the founder of the Tudor dynasty who became Henry VII. Adjacent to this town is Pembroke Dock, built by a vengeful Admiralty appalled by the unpatriotic raising of ship-repairing prices by Charles Grenville, owner of Milford across the harbour. Grenville created the town of Milford out of a fishing village as an economic experiment. The land was owned by Sir William Hamilton, husband of Nelson's Emma. She was herself "traded" by her protector, Hamilton's nephew Charles Grenville, a libertine gambler and ne'er-do-well who had lost a fortune at the gaming tables. He intended to recoup his fortune by making Milford a money-spinner. He invited Loyalist Quakers who had emigrated from the newly independent United States to New Brunswick and Nova Scotia, to return to Pembrokeshire and hunt sperm whales from Milford. These migrants enjoyed a brief prosperity which was terminated when sperm whale-oil for the street lighting of London was suddenly replaced by coal-gas. A further blow was given to the town's economy when Grenville, capitalizing on the long war with Napoleonic Europe and the extraordinary demands put upon the Royal Navy in its closing years, put up his ship-repairing prices. It was at this point that the Admiralty set up Pembroke Dock across the harbour and went on to build ships right through the nineteenth century until the coming of the *Dreadnought*. The Pembroke Dockyard built many of the first ironclads and all three Royal Yachts named *Victoria and Albert* were launched from its slips.

Despite the intrusions of its refineries, their piers, cracking towers, tank farms and flare-offs, Milford Haven is a beautiful harbour. Bleaker than Falmouth, for it is situated upon a weather-coast, the rich colour of its red rocks is also found in the soil of surrounding farmland. Its beaches are attractive, its villages delightful and it provided inspiration for the artist Graham Sutherland. Milford Haven was used by George IV as a port of embarkation for Ireland. In 1172 Henry II set out from Milford Haven with his Norman war-host to conquer Ireland. Whatever Henry's virtues as the architect of English Common Law, his military ambitions in Ireland have had dire and long-lasting consequences. But Milford Haven has not only seen the departure of kings with imperial ambitions overseas. It was also the landing place of a conqueror of England. Tucked just behind the headland of St Ann's lies the shallow indentation of Mill Bay. It was here, on 7 August 1485, that Henry Tudor, born in Pembroke Castle, landed at the head of his army of "base lackey Bretons" after a long exile in France. Having a claim to the English throne no better but not much worse than the Yorkists, this unwarlike and shrewd prince succeeded in destroying the last Plantagenet three weeks later on Bosworth Field. Upon the place of his landing he later dedicated a votive chapel to St Ann and it is on the site of this chapel that the present lighthouse stands.

Three lighthouses had been approved for construction on the west coast in 1662, but that at St Ann's was the only one ever built. It was to be supported by voluntary dues but some extortion seems to have been applied by the owners for in 1667 a complaint was received "of a Grievance on the People, by exacting an illegal Tax for maintaining a pretended Lighthouse at Milford Haven ...". Action was taken against the owners who had obtained money by coercion instead of on a voluntary basis. Obviously such a system could not work but, more extraordinarily, the solution was simply to discontinue the light! The tower was marked on contemporary charts as being "without fire" and not a single light burned on the west coast of England and Wales until the next century.

Following repeated petitions, a patent was at last issued to Trinity House in March 1713 and the Corporation concluded a lease with the landowner Joseph Allen to erect two coal-fired towers on the headland, their transit to lead ships clear of Linney Head. Allen built and lit the towers by the end of June 1714. He was empowered to levy one penny per ton on British shipping and two pence per ton on foreign vessels and he had to pay Trinity House £10 per annum for his ninety-nine year lease.

By the time Stevenson visited the lights in 1801 they held argand burners with parabolic reflectors. "Though they are about one hundred paces distant from each other there is a distinct *[sic]* keeper at each lantern, so that they are in the most complete state of cleanliness and good order!" Cliff erosion meant the rebuilding of the front light in 1841 and in 1910, with the installation of a red sector over the Crow Rock off Linney Head and the fitting of a flashing light in the front tower, the rear light was discontinued. It remains in use as a Coastguard Station. The front light was thoroughly modernized in 1958 and put on the mains, stand-by generators being maintained in case of a power failure in the National Grid. Today the station remains manned and forms an advanced base for helicopter operations to and from the remote lighthouses off the coast of west Pembrokeshire. Two of these three lights have already been converted to unmanned and automated operation, monitored from the base station at St Ann's, so that this, the first lighthouse to be illuminated on the west coast, may well be the last to be manned.

CHAPTER NINE

MERLIN'S LAND

Strumble Head.

From St Ann's Head the coast turns north, deeply indented at St Bride's Bay. The brilliant, much-folded, red sandstone swiftly gives way to grey silurian limestone. Off St Anne's, the island of Skokholm is a great slab of fissured red sandstone, its upper surface levelled by erosion and covered with short grass. Across Broad Sound and closer to the land lies another Viking-named island, Gateholm, which marks the end of this red rock. North of Skokholm, the larger island of Skomer is unprepossessingly dull, grey and lichen-covered. Around these islands lie fierce tidal races, dangerous in heavy weather, especially when wind and tide are in opposition.

Skokholm itself is about one and a half miles long. Although a string of rocks and reefs extends due west as far as the Smalls, there is a deep and wide channel immediately west of the island and, in 1916, an octagonal white lighthouse was built here to guide vessels through this inner passage. Now controlled from St Ann's, the 100,000-candela red light flashes from Skokholm every ten seconds and in thick or foggy weather the fog signal sounds every fifteen seconds. Formerly manned by three keepers as a "rock" station, Skokholm was quite civilized in comparison with some of the remote towers. The island is a bird reserve and usually had a small, sociable population of bird-watchers. The home of many species, Skokholm is especially noted for its breeding colonies of shearwaters and puffins. Both are burrow-nesting birds, occupying the abandoned warrens of rabbits. The Manx shearwater (confusingly named in Latin *puffinus puffinus*) is a dull-coloured pelagic bird with an oceanic range that stretches from the North to the South Atlantic. On land they shuffle awkwardly along, virtually immobile, only gaining grace in flight. Shearwaters skim low over the sea with almost motionless wings in search of the small fish, crustaceans and cephalopods that make up their diet. Almost silent at sea, they make a curious screaming and crooning sound at night in the breeding colonies. During the summer they often settle gregariously in large numbers on the sea, a habit known as "rafting".

A few miles west of Skokholm, there is another bird colony on the small brown island of Grassholm. This is inhabited solely by gannets and turns white during the summer from the numbers of birds and their droppings. A white cloud hangs over the island, where parent birds ridge-soar on the air currents rising over the land. The gannet is one of the loveliest of pelagic seabirds to be seen off our coasts. The young gannet swiftly grows to full size but then takes some four years to mature, starting its juvenile life with dark plumage which gradually whitens until the fully mature bird is a brilliant white with black wing tips and a

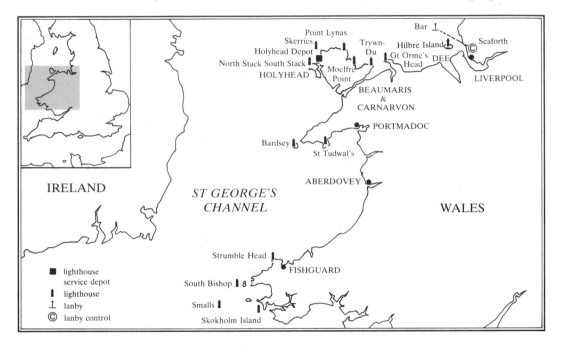

buff head patch. Gannets fly in small "platoons", covering vast distances in a "line ahead" formation, often very close to the water. However, they gain height to spot their prey and dive upon unsuspecting fish with half-closed wings and at a considerable speed. Male gannets are particularly aggressive when establishing or defending territory and often fight fiercely, each bird grasping the other's beak and trying to force it away. An adult gannet may possess a wing-span of six feet and they are usually on the wing, resting occasionally on the water.

Beyond Grassholm, lie the Hats and Barrels, dangerous reefs of resistant rock that claimed as their most recent victim the tanker *Christos Bitas*. The culmination of these rocky spurs is the Smalls, twenty miles west of the mainland. For more than two hundred years a lighthouse has stood upon the reef and its history is as interesting, if less dramatic, as that of the Eddystone. In 1763 an impoverished dock-master at Liverpool, John Phillips, conceived the idea of a light on the Smalls reef which lay off his native Welsh coast and which was a

St Ann's lighthouse stands on the site of a chapel said to have been built by Henry VII who landed in a cove close by the headland at the beginning of his invasion in 1485.

The jagged reef of the Skerries lies two miles offshore to the west of Carmel Head. The lighthouse was the last private light to come under the control of Trinity House.

danger much feared and talked of by the ship-masters entering the port of Liverpool. Despite the fact that Phillips was the agent for the Skerries lighthouse off Holyhead, his personal finances were insecure and he hovered on the edge of bankruptcy. But he eventually persuaded his creditors to advance more money, advertised for a lighthouse design and finally selected one submitted by Henry Whiteside. Whiteside had been born in Liverpool in 1748 but owned a business in London as "a maker of violins, spinettes and upright harpsichords". The projected lighthouse was to be of wood, an octagonal hut of two storeys, a living-room surmounted by the light-room. The hut sat on top of a lattice of timber baulks and three cast-iron struts supporting a central oak pile. The overall height was to be sixty-five feet and the spread of the legs about forty.

In the summer of 1775 Whiteside and Phillips set out from the tiny port of Solva on the northern arm of St Bride's Bay with a team of eight miners, a blacksmith and a couple of labourers. They had great difficulty in finding an anchorage, "the sea being turbulent and a gale of wind coming on suddenly". At the first attempt to work on the rock the boat had to stand off to avoid being smashed and five men were stranded. Although about twelve feet of rock are uncovered at high water, this is no protection against the height of even a low swell and their situation was perilous. By good fortune they had succeeded in driving one rod into the rock and were able to save themselves by clinging to this. On conclusion of the first season's work, an optimistically worded affidavit was signed for the benefit of Phillips's creditors and between June and October, "they missed no opportunity to do their utmost to accomplish the work they were sent to do: that in all this time they did not work . . . more in proportion to nine days, owing to the badness of the weather, and in part of that time six of the miners made one hole . . . for the central pillar, made a considerable progress in another, marked all the rest, and built a hut big enough to lodge twelve men and provision them for 14 days, which hut they one and all apprehend will maintain its station during the next winter . . ." During the winter Whiteside erected the whole structure at Solva. On discovering that the iron legs were faulty, he replaced them with oak timbers.

The summer of 1776 must have been mild for, although the hut had been lost, work went so well that the structure was set up and lights (green over white) shone out at dusk on 1 September. Perhaps even more remarkable, a cellar had been excavated in the rock to contain coal and a tank of fresh water. December gales, however, proved the building was rickety and in January 1770 Whiteside and his blacksmith arrived at the lighthouse to strengthen it. They were stranded with the keepers during severe gales and became short of food and water. Whiteside wrote for help, sealing three copies of his letter in three bottles and tossed them into the sea. By an almost incredible stroke of good fortune, one copy reached Thomas Williams, Phillips's agent, and Whiteside and his men were rescued. The keepers had, however, also run out of oil and the general condition of the tower, combined with its behaviour during the gales, persuaded Whiteside to abandon the light. In despair, Phillips surrendered his rights to his creditors, a group of Liverpool merchants. But the brief existence of the light, like David Avery's lightvessel at the Nore, had proved its value. Ship-masters approved of it enthusiastically and the Liverpool merchants now petitioned Trinity House. An Act of Parliament was passed in 1778, authorizing the Corporation to levy dues and repair the tower. In recognition of his services, Phillips was granted the lease at a peppercorn rent of £5 per annum and by September 1778 the light again shone forth. The tower had been strengthened and the bi-coloured light had been replaced with a new optic consisting of four reflectors, mounted at right angles to each other, five and a half feet in diameter that drew oil through wicks from a central reservoir and provided a steady white light.

A gruesome episode occurred in 1802 when one of the two keepers, Thomas Griffiths, died of natural causes while on duty at the lighthouse. His colleague, Thomas Howells, anxious to avoid any possible charge of murder, preserved the body outside the lantern until the boat arrived from Solva. It was three weeks before this happened, during which time the poor man lived with his grisly alibi. After this three men kept the light in the winter, two in the summer. The reflectors had to be replaced about 1812, possibly as a consequence of damage that occurred in October of that year. Whiteside described the accident in a letter to Stevenson:

"The misfortune that happened to the lighthouse was at first by the sea breaking some of the windows, at which the men were so much terrify'd, thinking that if the sea and wind together came into the room at one side and no passage out at the other the top would be carried away, and without further hesitation they set to and broke the remaining windows . . . It was a tremendous storm here such as cannot be remembered. The Smalls has now been up 37 years with no damage; only a few panes of glass broke sometimes. The men suffered very little hardships, only being frightened at the time of the storm."

The tower was abandoned a second time, but only until better weather in the spring of 1813 enabled the glass windows to be replaced. Further damage was done in 1831 when a sea smashed the sides and floor of the cabin. This time the cooking stove was squashed flat and the keepers were reduced to cooking over the argand burners.

In 1823 Trinity House tried cancelling the lease. Its acquisition of Flatholm at this time indicates the Corporation's desire to own more lighthouses itself and doubtless marks preliminary moves towards the 1836 Act. The annual profit for the Smalls was, by this time, reckoned at £7,000 per annum and the lessee's valuation was £148,430. This was considered excessive but when the Act was passed thirteen years later they were obliged to pay £170,468 for the remaining fifty-four years of unexpired term. Stevenson had disparagingly called Whiteside's tower "a raft of timber rudely put together" and dismissed Whiteside as a charlatan on the grounds that no mere instrument-maker could have any conception of how to build a lighthouse. Nevertheless, the rude raft survived for over eighty years, although requiring regular repairs and replacement of piles. Today the stumps of the original piles still survive, levelled with the rock. As we have seen, James Walker was sufficiently impressed with the performance of the tower to base his design for the original Bishop Rock lighthouse on Whiteside's concept.

In 1861 Nicholas and James Douglass built the present, magnificently proportioned tower to a design by James Walker. Painted red and white, the now familiar "tree bole" tower rises from a stepped base, intended to break up the seas and reduce their kinetic energy. The edges of these steps are as sharp now as when the Douglasses' masons hewed them out of the granite over a century ago. Today, after extensive alterations in the 1960s, a modern electric lamp uses the lens installed by Walker and is rated at one million candelas, throwing a white flash seaward three times every fifteen seconds. Due to the poor radar response given by a circular tower, the Supertyfon fog signal is augmented by a racon, indicating on a ship's radar screen the position of the lighthouse where it might otherwise be lost in the random echoes reflected off the waves beating over the reef, known as "sea-clutter". Considering the absence of any aids to navigation on the west coast until a surprisingly late date, the courage and persistence of both Phillips and Whiteside is to be admired. Several seamen have had cause to be grateful for the Smalls lighthouse as a refuge as well as for fixing their position. On 27 April 1876 the brigantine *Ellen Owen* of Newquay, Cardiganshire, was wrecked on the South-West Rock in dense fog. The crew managed to scramble ashore and were sheltered in the lighthouse until help arrived. The crew of the tug *Gulliver* of Greenock were similarly aided in June 1887. On 14 January of the same year the schooner *Redcliff* of Bristol left Milford at 5.00 p.m., bound for Waterford in Ireland. By 9.00 p.m. a gale had come on and the vessel ran on to the Barrels, a reef a few miles east of the Smalls. The crew took to the boat and at dawn on the 15th arrived off the lighthouse. Despite the very heavy sea that was running and at considerable risk to themselves, the keepers went down on the rocks and succeeded in rescuing the five men.

North of St Bride's Bay, a large number of rocks and islands stretch as far as St David's Head. Outriders of the Precelly Mountains from whose Silurian limestone distant Stonehenge is constructed, the tide sluices, racing through the sounds and guts that separate them. The main offshore island is Ramsey, supposedly once inhabited by the Breton holy man, Justinian. His saintly qualities imbued him with a desire for solitude and he took a sword and severed Ramsey from the mainland. A long row of jagged rocks known as The Bitches are the remains of his handiwork. He evidently attracted a following for his own death is reputed to have been due to these disciples, who, finding his disciplines too harsh, followed his example and cut off his head! Beyond Ramsey lie three rows of rocks known as the Bishops and Clerks. North and South Bishop are slightly isolated and their "clerks" appear to follow in an attendant row. Partly to mark this extremity, and also to indicate the inshore channel past Skokholm, a lighthouse was built on the South Bishop. Designed and completed in 1839 by James Walker, the station was electrified in 1969, and a helipad was added in 1971.

From behind Ramsey, in Whitesand Bay, St Patrick sailed to convert the Irish to Christianity. The bay is closed at its northern end by St David's Head, beyond which the coast falls back into the huge bight of Cardigan Bay, which is hardly used by shipping. Much of it is taken up by a missile range and it has only two lighthouses, one at Strumble Head marking the approach to Fishguard, the other away to the north on St Tudwal's island. Set on the small but precipitous islet of Ynys Michael, Strumble Head lighthouse was built in 1908 and automated in 1980. Like the South Bishop, it is a white tower, surrounded by a cluster of buildings set on a steep, brown-grey rock. Its cliffs are the haunt of many seabirds, including the rare red kite. Behind Strumble Head nestles Fishguard, the ferry port for Rosslare in the Irish Republic. Intended as the terminus of the Great Western Railway from which passenger ships would leave for America, Fishguard never realized this ambition which was usurped by Southampton. The *Mauretania* called once at the port but no regular sailings were ever established.

Fishguard has the dubious reputation of being the last place in the country to be invaded. In 1797 the French government landed the "Black Legion", a body of soldiers, paroled prisoners and ne'er-do-wells led by an Irish-American adventurer, Colonel Tate. Tate's orders were first to burn Bristol, then land in Wales and march on Chester and Liverpool. His troops were promised pardons for their crimes and all the plunder they could carry. Anchoring off Ilfracombe, a small party went ashore and burned a farm but, hearing of the approach of troops, hastily re-embarked and on 22 February landed at Fishguard. The local landowner, Lord Cawdor, called out the militia, yeomanry and volunteers and boldly advanced towards the invaders, whereupon Tate surrendered his 1,400 desperadoes to an inferior force "upon principles of humanity". He was also faced with a murderous mob of Welsh women who, with their red capes and black stovepipe hats, had at first been taken for infantry and were afterwards recognized as something far more formidable! Cawdor had to exercise his greatest efforts, not in out-manoeuvring Tate, but in preventing the women from murdering Frenchmen who had intended to commit rape.

Fishguard Bay is separated from its neighbour by Dinas Head, a huge, grey crag of a cliff which frowns down over the seascape. From here to Cemaes Head steep cliffs run, dropping sheer to the sea, interspersed by small ports once famous for their coasting schooners. Newquay was once said to have furnished more master mariners than any other place of comparable size in Britain. Dylan Thomas lived here for a while and may have created the memorable figure of Captain Haddock from one of these old shell-backs. Coasting northwards past Aberayron, the mountains draw back a little from the coast, which tends to become lower, due to the intrusion of several rivers. Aberystwyth, the cultural centre of modern Wales, grew up round the castle built by Edward I's brother Edmund Crouchback. It was captured by that renowned Welsh prince Owain

Glyndwr in 1404 and held against the English until recaptured by Prince Hal, the Monmouth Harry who went on to crown his military career at Agincourt. During the English Civil War it was loyal to the Royalist cause until besieged by the Parliamentary forces who pounded it into rubble.

A small, marshy coastal plain runs into sand across the wide estuary of the Dyfi, or Dovey. The northern shore of the River Dovey is backed by the flank of the North Wales Massif, a sudden hummocking of old, round-shouldered mountains that run north into Snowdonia. The Dyfi has "ponded back" to form a shallow lagoon while the river struggles seawards, over a sand-bar and out to sea. This difficult channel is used only by fishing and pleasure-craft, but is still buoyed by Trinity House. Splitting the mountains with its valley, the River Mawddach runs along the northern foothills of Cader Idris and, like the Dyfi, ponds back and debouches into Cardigan Bay with difficulty at Barmouth. The coastal passage north is barred by a long ridge of submarine rock, St Patrick's Causeway or the Sarn Badrig, but the mountains fall back round saltings and marsh below Harlech. Once protected by a creek, Harlech Castle was built between 1283 and 1289 by Edward I. Besieged by Madoc ap Llywelyn in 1294, the attack failed, as did an attack by Owain Glyndwr in 1401. By this time the whole of North Wales was in revolt against Henry IV and Harlech was beleagured. After four years the garrison were bribed to surrender to Glyndwr who held his court at Harlech until 1409 when it fell to an English army. In the Wars of the Roses Harlech held out in the Lancastrian cause and it was this stage that inspired the song *Men of Harlech*, the Earl of Pembroke's attacking force being called, somewhat misleadingly "Saxon foemen". Daffydd ap Ieuan surrendered to Pembroke on 14 August 1468.

North of Harlech, across the waters of Glaslyn, lies the town of Porthmadog. From this little port quantities of Welsh slate were once exported and one of the old trading vessels, the ketch *Garlandstone*, is preserved there. The town is named after the local MP, William Maddocks, who built a bund, known as The Cobb, to reclaim several thousand acres from the mudflats of the Afon Dwyryd. Beyond the coast the mountains rise, blue in the shimmer of a summer heat haze, mist-covered during the equinoctial gales, or white and frosted in the aftermath of a northerly wind. From Porthmadog the coast swings south-west and the green-hilled Lleyn peninsula reaches defiantly towards the Atlantic, terminating in the great open-jawed bay of Porth Neigwl, or Hell-mouth. Along the southern shore of the Lleyn, west of Criccieth, the ocean has dug deep into the land, but to leeward of the off-lying islands at the southern corner of the Lleyn, shallows extend to seaward and the volume of coastal trade warranted the building of a lighthouse on St Tudwal's West Island in 1877. In 1922 the keepers were removed, the dwellings sold and the station converted to automatic operation, using an acetylene-powered light. The lighthouse shines with both red and white sectors over the various rocks surrounding it.

The Lleyn peninsula is lower and greener than the Cambrian Massif. In the

Dark Ages of the fifth and sixth centuries AD it formed a remote refuge for the remnants of Romano-British culture. The area used to boast its own king, probably some vestigial Roman administrator. Off the western tip of the peninsula lies Bardsey Island whose headman was traditionally known as "king" right up to the beginning of this century. The island consists of a steep hill rising some six hundred feet almost sheer from the sea. The east side is precipitous, dropping into the deep water of Bardsey Sound, the channel that separates the island from the mainland. Through this channel the tide whirls and eddies, giving Bardsey its Welsh name, *Ynys Enlli*, the Isle of Eddies. The hill slopes more gently towards

The lighthouse on Bardsey Island.

the south and west, levelling to a narrow isthmus from which, quite flat, it opens out to the south where stands the red and white lighthouse. Known also as the "Island of Twenty Thousand Saints", Bardsey had a church as early as the third century AD. With the collapse of Roman civilization in the fifth century, it became a retreat. Pilgrims became refugees and many stayed, to be buried on the island. Whether there were twenty thousand of these remains a mystery! There is still a farm on the island and sheep graze on the hillside as well as the low pasture, but the population has dwindled since the turn of this century when it boasted a population of about one hundred. Merlin, Arthur's wizard, is said to have had his home on the island. If one accepts that Arthur was probably a Romano-British chieftan who, for a while, successfully stemmed the Saxon invasion, then it is not impossible that Merlin was an elderly, mendicant priest from Bardsey, possessed of certain skills that seemed wondrous to a rough army.

Bardsey lighthouse is unusual in that it is square in section. It was built privately in 1821 by Joseph Nelson and raised to increase its visible range in 1910. Today the station has a powerful group flashing white light, giving five brilliant flashes every fifteen seconds. It is also fitted with a racon, and is floodlit at night.

The island is better named by the Welsh. Tides in Bardsey Sound run at up to five knots and swirl through the two-mile-wide gap with amazing energy. The summit of Bardsey is often lost in mist and cold air can descend rapidly in violent katabatic squalls, hazardous to yachts. The poet and yachtsman Hilaire Belloc describes such an experience in *The Cruise of the "Nona"*:

> But what happened was something wholly unexpected; it is always so at sea . . . with the rising of the sun it blew hard . . . we shortened down to three reefs, but even so the helm was pulling hard, and when we changed jibs and put up the smallest we had, it griped more than I liked, straining my arm . . . The gale rose higher and the sea with it; but, tearing through the water as we now were under three reefs . . . the dinghy had to be abandoned. The tide against us was so fierce that even under that gale we hardly moved; and it was strange to see, from the leaping and the struggling of the *Nona*, as the foam rushed by in a millrace, how steady remained the points on the Carnarvonshire shore, and how slowly we opened the Sound . . . All the while the wind howled and the sea continued to rise and to boil in a cauldron more violent as the gale on the one hand and the tide against it on the other grew in strength, and in the fierceness of their struggle. In seas like this one never knows when some great tumbling lump of water may not break upon one's decks, for there is no run and follow, it is all confusion; and I remember thinking as I took the helm again in the midst of the turmoil of something I had seen written once of Portland Race: "The sea jumps up and glares at you" – a sound phrase.

From Braich-y-Pwll the coast of the Lleyn trends north-eastwards to form the bight of Carnarfon Bay. The igneous spine of the peninsula falls more gently to the sea on its northern flank. Pre-Cambrian and Palaeozoic rocks form outcrops, but the intervening beaches are long and beautiful. At Porthnor the tiny grains of sand "squeak" when walked upon. Along this lovely coast medieval pilgrims made their way to Bardsey in hope of grace. It is a measure of Bardsey's sanctity that three pilgrimages to its shrines were held to equal one to Rome. Medieval culture also revived and embellished the legend of Arthur, and it was soon asserted that after the defeat and death of Arthur, Merlin had concealed a great treasure on the island.

To the north-west of Bardsey, Porth Dinllaen was briefly considered as a site for the terminus of the Irish packet service, but Telford's road, and later the railway, ran to Holyhead instead, and the Lleyn peninsula was allowed to remain remote and beautiful. It enjoyed a brief prominence during the wars between Edward I and the house of Llywelyn ap Iorwerth, for it was on level land near Porth Dinllaen that the Norman Edward held his great triumphant tournament in 1284 after the defeat and death of Llywelyn ap Gruffydd.

The north of Carnarfon Bay is formed by the southern coast of Anglesey. This island is separated from the mainland by the narrow Menai Strait. Geologically complex, the Strait is formed from the flooded valleys of three rivers. Tides ebb and flood through it with a destructive rapidity, and those small ships that still navigate its waters do so with the utmost caution. The south-east corner of Anglesey is heavily wooded, planted with the tall and erect Corsican Pine. It is a flat land compared with the heights of Snowdonia. The coast is low, rock outcroppings alternating with small, intimate and delightful beaches. The flooded valley of the Cefni River was another site from which land was reclaimed from the sea, this time by the great eighteenth-century road builder, Robert Telford (1757-1834).

A narrow and shallow strait divides Holy Island from Anglesey. The coast remains flat, then rises steeply to the slopes of Holyhead Mountain. The great breakwater that enclosed Holyhead Harbour was quarried from its slopes and, although less than eight hundred feet high, its summit commands stunning views in clear weather. In exceptional conditions, Ireland and the Isle of Man are visible, but Holyhead is in the track of the great weather-brewing depressions and liable to heavy mist and orographic cloud. Two spurs of the mountains run precipitously into the Irish Sea at the North and South Stacks. There the water is very deep, up to the foot of the stacks themselves, but their prominence, forced out into the tide-waters that ebb and flow round Anglesey to the huge bight of Liverpool Bay, ensure that a swift flow is felt beneath the cliffs which can swiftly become a race.

A fog signal station is situated on the North Stack, operated remotely from the Corporation's depot at Holyhead and on the South Stack a magnificent white lighthouse stands sentinel. Built in 1809 by David Alexander, the ninety-foot tower seems ridiculously far below the vertical cliffs behind it, yet its height was calculated exactly to avoid the orographic shroud commonly found overhead. Early attempts to obtain a patent to build a lighthouse on the South Stack had been unsuccessful. It seems to have been Trinity House itself that eventually obtained sanction and built the lighthouse on its own account. Alexander's tower cost £12,000, the materials being run across the chasm separating the stack from the mountain by an aerial runway of hemp rope. This runway remained in use for many years for the transport of stores, materials and personnel. Oil lamps and reflectors were fitted on completion of the building and in 1818 the Deputy Master, Sir Joseph Cotton, claimed that the light was "never obscured by clouds". Fog, however, was a different matter and a curious railway was later

The lighthouse on the island of Stokholm is now controlled from St Ann's. The island is a bird reserve, especially noted for its colonies of shearwaters and puffins.

Top: The peaceful village of Abersoch on the Lleyn peninsula is now a centre for powerboat enthusiasts as well as for sailing boats. Above: St Tudwal's Islands are two rocky islets that lie off the south coast of the Lleyn peninsula. The lighthouse on the west island has been an automatic station since 1922.

The lighthouse on South Stack, a tiny island off the north-west tip of Holy Island, was built in 1809 by David Alexander who was also the architect for Dartmoor Prison.

*The South Bishop lighthouse was built by James Walker
in 1839 both to mark the extremity of a line of jagged
rocks and to indicate the inshore channel past Stokholm.*

installed, down which a subsidiary lantern was lowered in foggy weather. As deep water runs all the way to the cliff, a ship navigating on soundings would have no prior warning that she was approaching danger until she hit the cliffs.

In 1828 an iron suspension bridge was slung across the turbulent gut which lasted until 1964 when the present aluminium one was constructed. On Tuesday, 25 October 1859 a violent gale blew up, known ever afterwards as the "*Royal Charter* Gale". Named after a ship wrecked in the storm, the *Royal Charter* was only one of some two hundred vessels that were wrecked, stranded or seriously damaged in the storm. Even the South Stack lighthouse was not immune. Crossing the iron suspension bridge during the night at the height of the gale, assistant keeper Jack Jones was struck on the head by a boulder torn from the cliff above. Jones dragged himself across the bridge, bleeding and concussed, finally collapsing on the path up to the lighthouse. Henry Bowen, the principal keeper, assuming that Jones was unable to relieve him in the gale that was howling across the bridge, remained at his post until morning and only then saw the body of the unfortunate Jones. He ran to his mate's assistance and found Jones groaning and incoherent, his hair matted with blood and quite unable to move. He died three weeks later of a compound fracture of the skull.

The lighting apparatus of the South Stack was renewed about 1876 and in 1909 an early form of incandescent burner was fitted. This was renewed in 1927 and then replaced by electric power in 1938. Today the station runs off the National Grid but with stand-by generators in case of any power failure. The modern optic generates two and a half million candelas and emits a white flash every ten seconds; the station is now remotely controlled from the Corporation's depot at Holyhead. Access to the suspension bridge is down four hundred steps cut in the mountainside. Descending these is a remarkable sensation, giving an insight into the life of a seabird, for one is surrounded by ridge-soaring gulls and kittiwakes, all riding the air as it rushes up the cliff-face. Guillemots and razor-bills whirr off the rock ledges, their rapid wing beats adapted for both flight and underwater swimming. Jackdaws and the rare chough with its brilliant red bill and legs can be seen on this western-facing slab of rock and so can that bird of ancient magic, the raven. Before Poe traduced it, this largest of the crows with its spectacular aerial courtship displays, this plunderer of nests and eater of carrion, might have been the black familiar of Merlin himself.

Tucked beneath the frowning mass of the grey mountain is the town of Holyhead. In Welsh *Caergybi*, the fortress of Cybi, a local saint, it was founded by the legions of Rome in the third century. Today the ferries to Ireland from here connect with the long railway line from London and the road begun by the Roman military authorities and finished by Telford. Trinity House retains a sub-depot in the port, of particular value as a helicopter back-up base and buoy storage area.

From Holyhead the coast runs north; rolling farmland is fronted by sandy beaches and rock outcrops. The land rises to rocky cliffs at Carmel Head where it turns due east, a trend which continues as far as the estuary of the Dee and the English border. Lying off Carmel Head, are a number of islets, reefs and isolated rocks. The most prominent of these is the jagged reef of the Skerries, a word deriving from the Gaelic *sgeir*, a rock. Attempts to build a lighthouse here were unsuccessful until 1705, when a Captain John Davison presented a petition to the Attorney-General. Such was the grinding pace of the bureaucracy that it was 1709 before the petition received the attention of Trinity House. Surprisingly for the period, the Elder Brethren agreed a lighthouse was needed and undertook the responsibility themselves. They were astonished when the Attorney-General decided that Davison should build it instead. Davison, however, was unable to raise the capital and in 1713 the Skerries were bought by a wealthy Liverpool merchant named William Trench. Trench quickly obtained a patent and the following year sent his son and six workmen off to survey the site. Sadly all seven men were lost when the boat was wrecked. To his credit, Trench persisted and in 1717, at a cost of £3,000, the tower was completed and on "ye 4th November a fire was kindled therein and ever since supported". Trench had few constructional problems, for the highest point of the reef is well above high water. The original keeper's dwelling with its characteristic stepped gable-end remains in use today as a store. It was here one night that the keeper and his wife were disturbed by a sudden knocking on the door. Thinking that this was the effect of the gale then blowing, neither took much notice until it occurred again. The husband went to open the door, his wife stood somewhat apprehensively behind him. As the keeper threw open the door the full roar of the gale struck them, blowing through the coals high above them and filled the night with a diabolical, orange light. The air was filled with flying spray and the rocks shook with the impact of the seas. The shadows leapt across the rocks that the God-fearing couple thought they had to themselves. Suddenly the naked figure of a negro was illuminated, the only survivor from a ship that had been wrecked on the reef without their knowledge! Thinking that she had seen the devil, the keeper's wife passed out!

Light dues for the lighthouse proved difficult to collect. When Trench died in 1729, largely ruined by the expenses incurred in maintaining the Skerries, his daughter sold out. However, the issue was laid before Parliament and the lease was reconferred on Trench's family. In 1804 the tower was largely rebuilt under the supervision of Trinity House. Twenty-two feet were added to its height, the parapet ennobled by battlements; argand oil lamps and reflectors were then installed behind a glass lantern. By 1834 the lighthouse was netting an annual profit of £12,000, due largely to the growth of Liverpool and the regular collection of dues. This had not gone unnoticed by Parliament who, at the time of passing their special Act in 1804, had made a special annual grant of £1,700 to the proprietors for out-of-pocket expenses. By this time the Skerries was owned by a shrewd Welshman named Morgan Jones and it was revelations like this that precipitated the 1836 Act. When the Act received the Royal Assent, Jones refused the compensation as being insufficient, but he died in 1841 before the matter was resolved. His executors insisted the matter be put before a jury who rejected Trinity House's offer and settled upon the unbelievable sum of £444,984! The Skerries was, in fact, the last private light to come under Trinity House's control. Converted to self-generated electrical power in 1927, the station was further modernized in 1967. The power of the modern optic is of four million candelas intensity giving a group of two flashes every ten seconds. A red sector is thrown over the reefs off Carmel Head and a powerful diaphone sounds in poor visibility.

Carmel Head once bore a semaphore station upon its summit. Financed by the wealthy shipping houses of Liverpool, a message took about seven minutes to transmit, via the stations on Mynydd Eilian, Puffin Island, the Great Orme, Hilbre Island in the Dee and Bidston Hill. The arrival of ships approaching the port was often of crucial interest to ship-owners and their clients, and the news often played a crucial role in their bartering for options on cargoes and gambling on the market prices of all manner of commodities.

Rounding Carmel Head, the nuclear power station at Wylfa stands grey and block-like amid rolling green farmland. East of Wylfa is the indentation of Cemaes Head and at Amlwch Shell Oil maintain a Mono-buoy, at once a mooring and a discharging line connected ashore to a pipeline running beneath the ground. Amlwch prospered as a ship-building port and an exporter of copper from the mines in the Parys Mountain. At the beginning of the last century annual exports of copper reached 80,000 tons before competition from American mines forced them to close.

At Point Lynas the coast swings south-eastward, trending inwards towards the northern end of the Menai Strait. The rise of Liverpool during the latter half of the eighteenth century lasted until a little after half-way through the present century. In its heyday the mercantile community of the city built their own lighthouses along the coast of North Wales. Anxious to have them on the Isle of Man as well, they were unwilling either to undertake the construction of such lights, or to put up with the frequent poor service given by private lights (that at the Skerries being a case in point). There was also the vexatious problem of the payment of light-dues which were considered, at least in England, to be higher than the variable quality of lights could justify. It was, therefore, to the Commissioners of Northern Lighthouses that they applied for help at the beginning of the nineteenth century. The Scottish engineer Robert Stevenson was only too glad to oblige and the lighthouses on Man remain the responsibilty of the Northern Lighthouse Board to this day.

The coast of North Wales forms much of the approach to Liverpool and at Point Lynas, the Liverpool port authorities themselves set up a lighthouse and pilot station. During the last quarter of the eighteenth century the harbour master at Liverpool was William Hutchinson, an experienced seaman who had sailed in both merchant ships and armed privateers and had been in command himself. In 1777 he published *Practical Seamanship* which is still full of good advice and for twenty years he meticulously observed the tides for computing predictions. Being of an experimental and scientific turn of mind, Hutchinson made a number of innovations at the port, in particular constructing a number of lighthouses and introducing new means of illuminating them. Point Lynas was the site of one such light. Although occupied earlier as a pilot-lookout and boarding-station where pilots sailed out to incoming ships to offer their services for the approach to the Mersey, it was 1779 before a proper lighthouse was built, using Hutchinson's own design of burners and reflectors. In 1835 the present light

Storm Force 11.

was built, a low, white, castellated tower connected to the pilot station. Fully automated now, the mains power is supported by the usual stand-by services. The fog-signal is triggered by a fog detector which operates if visibility drops below two and a half miles. Escaping the 1836 Act, since the light was owned by a public and not a private body, ownership passed from the Liverpool Town Council (then the port authority) to the Mersey Docks and Harbour Board in 1879. The lighthouse passed to the Corporation of Trinity House in 1973, although the Mersey pilots still operate from the adjacent pilot station and their smart, fast cutters put pilots on board and take them off ships inward and outward from the port of Liverpool.

Near Point Lynas is the little village of Moelfre. Moelfre possesses one of the most distinguished lifeboat stations in Britain that in its century and a half of existence has saved about a thousand lives. In October 1959 its coxswain, Richard Evans, added a second gold medal to his outstanding achievements by taking the eight-man crew off the coaster *Hindlea* in appalling weather. Exactly a century earlier, during the "*Royal Charter* Gale" in which assistant keeper Jack Jones lost his life at the South Stack lighthouse, the iron sailing ship *Royal Charter* was homeward bound from Australia for Liverpool. On board were about four hundred and fifty people, most of them gold-miners and their families, returning from the gold-fields of New South Wales with about half a million pounds worth of gold. Attempting to round Point Lynas and shelter at anchor in Redwharf Bay, she struck rocks near Moelfre and began to break up. One of her seamen swam ashore with a rope to where would-be rescuers had gathered on the low cliff-top. The Moelfre lifeboat was launched and between the breeches-buoy that was rigged up using the rope and the gallantry of the lifeboat, about a dozen people were rescued before the *Royal Charter* broke her back and began to go to pieces in the monstrously heavy sea that was pounding her. By dawn more than four hundred men, women and children had perished. Much of the gold has been recovered but the wreck remains an attraction for Scuba divers.

Redwharf Bay, which the *Royal Charter* had been making for, has been formed by the sea eating into the dipping folds of the rock strata that run from the north-east to the south-west throughout the area. (A contrasting upward fold forms the Lleyn peninsula.) The eastern end of the bay is formed of carboniferous rocks, a contrast to pre-Cambrian formations elsewhere on Anglesey. Off this north-east corner, shoals, rocks and islands clutter the northern entrance to the Menai Strait. The point of entry is marked by the automatic lighthouse on Trwyn Du (Black Nose). Formerly a manned station, the black and white lighthouse was built in 1832 on a spur of rock that juts out from the beach and covers at half tide. It was converted to unwatched status in 1922 and it has an automatic bell as a fog signal.

The opposite side of the entrance is marked by a large stone beacon, bright red and painted annually by the crew of the tender. This is built on a rocky spur extending south from Puffin Island. Puffin Island was once home to a large colony of puffins but is now over-run with rats. On its spiny summit are the ruins of St Seiriol's monastery, some fourteen centuries old. Saint Seiriol was supposed to know a secret route over the sands that choke the Strait to the eastward and he established a number of other religious houses nearby. Seen from Puffin Island, Snowdonia rises magnificently from its foothills across the water. The town of Conwy on its winding river disappears in a cleft in these hills. Marked by Trinity House, this tortuous channel is now used mainly by yachts and fishing craft. Dominating the estuary, the immense rocky hummock of the Great Orme rises massive and grey, a great fist of carboniferous limestone smashed down into the sea. Slightly lower than Holyhead's mountain, the precipitous nature of its seaward face gives a greater impression of height. Beneath its eastern flank the holiday centre of Llandudno huddles under its lee.

Upon the Great Orme is another of the lighthouses once owned by the Port of Liverpool. Built in 1862 and taken over by Trinity House in 1973, it is a white, castellated, almost Gothic building, set just below the summit of the rock to avoid cloud. The diminishing trade of Liverpool caused this lighthouse to be discontinued in 1985. The extensive shoals of the Chester Flats which lie to the eastward of the Great Orme choke the mouth of the Dee and lie off the low coast of North Wales. The River Dee reaches the sea between the Flint coast and the Wirral peninsula, through a maze of ever-shifting sandbanks. There are occasional deep holes, like Wild Road off the Point of Air, but the navigation is restricted to the upper half of the tide for the small sea-going ships that make for Mostyn and the other small ports of the Dee. Entered from the west, vessels have to negotiate the Rhyl and Hoyle Banks and the Chester Bar before rounding the disused lighthouse on the Point of Air and sailing into the river proper. A secondary channel runs from the north, bending tortuously round Hilbre Island to join the first at the Point of Air. The Dee is a river in a state of nature, wild, unpredictable and possessing an atmosphere all its own. Well marked by buoys, the approaches to the tiny ports of Flint and Mostyn echo the common characteristics of the majority of estuaries on the coast. There are fierce tides and extensive, shifting banks, their exits challenged by the sea itself so that they are choked by sand-bars and difficult to navigate. But the Dee possesses them on the grand scale and its abrupt and unpredictable changes have destroyed the tenuous prosperity of its little ports, often at a stroke.

The Chester Flats are formed of glacial deposits that form a "terrace" along the littoral which has encouraged the growth of holiday resorts at Rhyl and Prestatyn. Beyond them the green and rounded hills rise to be lost in the distance. But beneath the old, disused lighthouse on the Point of Air lies a coal field whose pithead winding gear marks the abrupt transition from seaside to industrialized foreshore. The south bank of the Dee, along which the deepest channel of the river runs, is dismally industrialized as it fades south-east into the distance. The magic of Merlin's Britain is gone. The horizon is dominated now, to the east and north, by the sadly decaying industrial heartland of England.

CHAPTER TEN
THE NORTH-WEST

St Bees.

The rock beds of the Wirral peninsula close with the opposite shore of Lancashire and force the River Mersey to scour its own bed along the seven miles of waterfront that form the dockland areas of Liverpool and Birkenhead. This was the chief reason for Liverpool superseding Chester as the major port for the region. The western end of the Wirral is terraced, allowing sand to accumulate so that the old channels that linked the Dee and the Mersey are now silted up completely. It was to guide ships through these channels that William Hutchinson built his lighthouses in the 1760s. Today the old towers at New Brighton, Leasowe and Bidston Hill remain, but are unlit. Leasowe lighthouse, on the sandy foreshore at Hoylake, was built after a ship-wreck in 1760. The vessel broke up and her cargo of cotton bales was dumped in the sand. It was soon found that the bales bound the moving dunes long enough for marram grass to become established and on the resulting firm ground Hutch-inson built his lighthouse.

The advantage conferred on Liverpool by the deep water running alongside its banks was consolidated in the years that followed Hutchinson's death, by the excavating of an ever-increasing series of docks, cuts and locks on both sides of the river. Depth of water was preserved and kept constant in the approaches by the building of training walls, rough lines of boulders which confined the river to a predetermined path and used its own scour to keep the channel clear. Liverpool became a fabulously wealthy port and by 1880 forty per cent of the world's trade was carried in Liverpool ships. The port authority became wealthy enough not only to have its own lighthouses and a lightvessel at the Liverpool Bar, but to own its own yacht, the *Galatea*, purchased, curiously, from Trinity House. Today Liverpool has been abandoned by the tide of commerce. Despite the modern container terminal at Formby, Liverpool is suffering from a variety of ills. The end of imperial trade and the decline of the British Merchant Navy, the demise of the general-cargo ship and the shift to containerization, the dwindling of British exports and the shift of commercial emphasis to European markets have all had their part to play. But other factors have hastened this decline, most notably the rise of the national flag fleets of the Third World and the superior viability of the great European entrepôts of Rotterdam and Hamburg. The ulcers of recession have broken out all round the coast – on the Tyne, the Tees, at Southampton and the ports of South Wales. But nowhere are they as bad as at Liverpool.

The channel into the Mersey remains the responsibility of the port and it is serviced by Liverpool's own buoy tender, the motor vessel *Vigilant*. This fairway follows the northern bank before turning west to the Bar and the Irish Sea, the

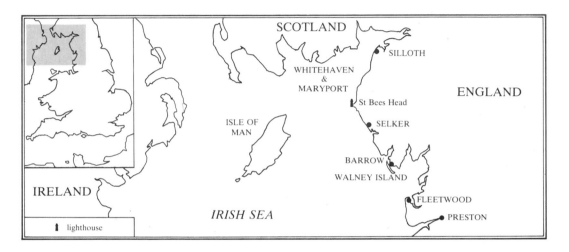

training wall separating it from the extensive sands and dunes which fringe the shoreline at Blundellsands. These sands extend many miles to seaward so that navigation is not possible close along the shore. A port that has accepted the kiss of death is neighbouring Preston, situated on the River Ribble.

At Lytham St Anne's the coast continues north, again fronted by miles of shallow water and golden sands. The Lytham lifeboat is another station with a history of tragedy. In 1886 both the Lytham and Southport lifeboats were launched to go to the assistance of the German barque *Mexico*. Both boats got into difficulties themselves, all hands were lost from the Lytham boat and only two escaped from the Southport lifeboat. This double disaster spurred on greater efforts to perfect a self-righting lifeboat. Behind the sands of Blackpool and its conspicuous tower, the Fylde peninsula stretches away to the eastward, to merge with the distant blue slopes of the Pennines. The Fylde terminates at Rossal Point, a flat, barely noticeable headland, almost inconspicuous but for the power station and buildings of Fleetwood. Running north just behind the point the River Wyre gouges its way through the banks to join the fast running and tidally invaded River Lune whose estuary carves a very deep trench through the sand and mud that choke Morecambe Bay. Although miles of sand and shallow water fringe the low-lying, marshy coast, the area is seamed with apparently aimless and surprisingly deep pits, abbreviated channels leading nowhere that are probably the remains of earlier fairways. Coach tracks were once known across the sands, avoiding the tedious detour round the head of the bay, but it is desolate, more reminiscent of Essex than that of a flooded valley between the Pennines and the mountains of the Lake District. There are outcrops of old, worn rock, like Humphrey Head, dividing the upper bight of Morecambe Bay, where the last wolf in England is reputed to have been killed, but the shore mainly consists of sea walls and salt marsh, a paradise for waders, duck, geese and the rare bittern.

The River Wyre, which forms the fairway into Fleetwood, emerges just within the confines of Rossal Point. Buoyed locally, the channel is also marked by an old, disused pile lighthouse that stands on the sands which flank it. Fleetwood's once famous fleet of Arctic trawlers that fished the distant waters of Iceland, the Davis Strait and the White Sea, have been destroyed by cod wars and the "go-it-alone" policies of successive governments. East of the Wyre, the Rivers Lune and Kent lead to Lancaster and Heysham, while Morecambe itself commands a fine stretch of sand beyond, boasting landladies as famous as their competitors at Blackpool. Morecambe Bay was formerly the centre of a large shrimping fishery. Special boats were built locally and were probably the most yacht-like work-boats built in this country during the last years of sail. Known as "Nobbies" they were designed to operate in shallow water where wind and tide combined to throw up a steep, short sea. The constraints of handling nets required a low-freeboard so they had a round, spoon bow, low hull and long, elliptical counter stern. In order to assist them over a foul tide, they carried a lot of sail, being rigged as gaff-cutters, but their bowsprits were unstayed and their masts a single pole for simplicity. Their design was so successful that they operated as far south as Cardigan Bay. The shrimps were caught using a beam net from the starboard side and promptly boiled on board in a "Dutch pot" which belched smoke conspicuously. A few remain as yachts and one is being restored at the Exeter Maritime Museum.

On the far side of the bay, beyond Humphrey Head, the Rivers Crake and Leven run off the foothills of Cumbria. On Hoad Hill above Ulverston stands a stone replica of Smeaton's Eddystone lighthouse, an extraordinary monument to a local-boy-made-good. Born in June 1764, John Barrow was the son of a small-holder who attracted the notice of the local curate who ran Ulverston Grammar School. Finding in Barrow some mathematical ability, this worthy man encouraged his protégé and obtained employment for him as an itinerant maths teacher, the surveyor of an estate and a post as tutor to a midshipman older than himself. Barrow was then offered a job as accountant for a family owning a small iron-foundry in Liverpool which he accepted. When the owner died, Barrow shipped aboard a whaler bound for Spitzbergen and the lure of the Arctic was to last him a lifetime. On the whaler's return, he obtained a job in Greenwich, teaching maths under the eye of the Astronomer Royal, Neville Maskelyne. Among his pupils were many sons of influential men, including Lord Anson, then enjoying high office at the Admiralty. Barrow was given a more lucrative post as tutor to the son of Sir George Staunton through which he met Lord Macartney. When Macartney led his famous embassy to the Emperor of China in 1792, Barrow was one of his secretariat and, five years later, after the outbreak of the French Revolutionary War when the Cape of Good Hope had been taken from the Dutch, Barrow accompanied its new governor, Lord Macartney, to Cape Town. There he became an authority on African and Chinese affairs, publishing a number of books before returning to Britain at the Peace of Amiens. In 1804 Lord Melville took office as First Lord of the Admiralty and appointed John Barrow as Second Secretary in which capacity he remained (except for a break during the Whig administration of 1806-7) until his retirement in 1845. He served four sovereigns, thirteen governments and forty Admiralty Boards through much of the longest naval war in British history, "a wise and friendly administrator". He was also a figure in the contemporary literary world, a friend of John Murray, a contributor to the *Quarterly Review*, the *Encyclopaedia Britannica* and the author of biographies of Lord Howe and Peter the Great. His *The Eventful History and Piratical Seizure of HMS Bounty* remains a classic. He became a baronet in 1835, was a founder of the Royal Geographical Society and a Fellow of the Royal Society. At the end of the long war with France he suggested St Helena as a suitable place for the victorious allies to mew up Napoleon, and then turned his energies to the encouragement of Arctic exploration by the brilliant young naval officers who had had their expectations of glory cut short by the end of the war. He was honoured by the men he inspired who gave his name to the strait between Baffin Bay and the Beaufort Sea, part of the North-West Passage whose discovery he worked so hard to encourage. It was possibly because of Barrow's luminary qualities in this field that a lighthouse was considered an apt subject for his monument.

Whilst the tide rushes ferociously in and out of the Lune Deep, it meanders with far less vigour over the Lightning Knoll, a few miles to the north, at the entrance to the fairway leading to Barrow-in-Furness. Indeed the expanse of shallow water seems to discourage the building of great ships, yet the cranes on the distant skyline, behind the sandy beach and white pile of the lighthouse on Walney Island proclaim otherwise. Buoyed by the port authority, leading beacons indicate the approach channel which swings north, inside the low prominence of Walney Island and into the Barrow Channel to the building yards and the docks. The fairway passes Piel Island which is thought to have been first fortified by the Danes. The island possesses a remarkably fine castle keep which is visible from seaward and was built in 1327. Piel Island is famous for having been the starting point of Lambert Simnel's abortive invasion of England in 1486.

It is past this flat little pancake of an island with its ancient keep that the most destructive single machine of war ever devised passes from its place of creation to the ocean. Barrow-in-Furness has been the birthplace of British warships since iron finally ousted timber and it is here that Britain's nuclear-powered and nuclear-armed submarines are constructed. Ironically the Cistercian monks of Furness Abbey were the first to smelt iron hereabouts. At the outset of the industrial revolution, little smelting was done locally, most of the ore mined in Furness being shipped to the iron-towns of South Wales, but in 1846 a railway connection was laid between Barrow and the mines at Dalton. There was an immediate increase in production which the following year rose to a staggering 50,000 tons. Even so, the population of Barrow was still less than four hundred. In the following years, the rail network expanded and in 1859 Schneider and

Walney Island provides the shelter which makes Barrow-in-Furness a perfect natural harbour.

Hannay's iron works was established in Barrow, being absorbed in 1866 by the Barrow Haematite Steel Company which used Bessemer's process to boost output. Other industries followed iron and steel production, the first ship being built in 1873 and rapidly Barrow became a well established shipbuilding area. Although both naval and merchant vessels have been constructed, the Vickers yard has specialized in the construction of warships, particularly submarines.

To the north of the Furness peninsula, a smaller version of Morecambe Bay exists where the sea has flooded the mouth of the River Duddon. Duddon Sands is a vast yellow plain of level golden sand at low water, a paradise for thousands of waders, duck and geese. The invasion of the sea has blurred the margins of the land, turning them into salt-marsh, although the whole inlet is surrounded by the mountains of Cumbria and the Lake District. From the low sandy shore of Haverigg Point the land quickly rises to cliffs. There is only one break in this west-facing escarpment, at Drigg Point where the Rivers Esk, Mite and Irt pour into the sea after converging at Ravenglass. Between Haverigg Point and Drigg Point the heights of Black Combe tower over the coast, inhospitably confining the habitations of men to the narrowing coastal strip. But the distant hills are not all forbidding. Although from the sea nothing can be seen of the lakes that give

The lighthouse on St Bees headland stands on the only cliffs on the shores of Cumbria. It is the last lighthouse before the Scottish border.

their name to the area and inspired the "Swallows and Amazons" stories of Arthur Ransome, there are distantly wistful views of the little white farms that Beatrix Potter depicted so beautifully. Sca Fell and Great Gable and far Helvellyn lend a superb grandeur to this section of the coast. Beyond the reef known as the Selker Rocks, the remains of an old headland and the only impediment to navigation along this stretch of coast, the gaunt, uncompromising bulk of the nuclear plants at Sellafield form an unlovely contrast with the mountains. In 1956 Britain's first nuclear power station was built at Calder Hall, changing its name later to Windscale. The whole complex is now known as Sellafield and incorporates the nuclear fuel reprocessing plant which has long been the subject of fierce and partisan controversies. To a seaman, it seems that any solution should give priority to the preservation of the environment.

The foreshore, which drops itself to beach level to allow the little Rivers Annas, Ehen and Calder to run into the sea, begins to climb again, steepening into cliffs over two hundred feet high at St Bees Head. The headland is a great knuckle stuck out into the Irish Sea, a lonely, isolated spot, ideal for the contemplative life. The promontory was named after St Bega, an Irish princess who vowed to devote her life to holiness and founded a convent, built just behind the headland. The house was destroyed in a Viking raid, but was re-established by Norman Benedictines in 1120. Beyond the point the land falls away, giving ground to the Solway Firth and the border country, so St Bees is also the ideal site for a lighthouse.

In 1718 Trinity House obtained a patent and granted a lease to Thomas Lutwige for a term of ninety-nine years at a rent of £20 per annum. Lutwige undertook to build and maintain a lighthouse on St Bees for which he was empowered to levy dues of three-halfpence a ton on shipping at the neighbouring ports of Whitehaven, Maryport and Workington. The tower he built consisted of an untidy-looking buttressed masonry edifice with keepers' dwellings incorporated into the base. Keepers were engaged at seven shillings a week and they ascended the tower by means of a numer of ladders, so placed as to avoid the wind-driven smoke. This does not say much for the quality of the light which appears to have been from a fire lit in an iron brazier, suspended from a gallows. The Scottish lighthouse engineer Stevenson was unimpressed on his visit in 1801: "St Bees light is from coals exposed upon the top of an old tower in an open chauffer, which is at the top only two feet diameter, at bottom one foot six inches and two feet deep; so that in storms so small a body of fire cannot be kept up as it ought to be. About one hundred and thirty tons of coal are said to be used annually." In 1814 the Royal Academician, William Daniell, made a sketch of the almost ruined building and wrote that it was "of the meanest description and provided with a very bad light supplied by a coal fire. I imagine a light in this situation is admitted to be of very little use or such a one as this could not scarcely be submitted to or escape the vigilant observation of the Trinity House." Whether or not St Bees had escaped the "vigilant observation" of the Elder Brethren is not known. Probably the light was considered adequate to serve the coastal ports a few miles away, for the coal chauffer lingered on to become the last used in Britain, until the tower caught fire in 1822. It was William Hutchinson who described the virtual uselessness by the 1760s of open coal lights still in use. "Open coal fire light, exposed to all winds and weathers, cannot be made to burn and show a constant steady blaze to be seen at a sufficient distance . . . for in storms of wind, when lights are most wanted, these open fires are made to burn furiously . . . so as to melt the very ironwork about the grate, and in cold weather, when it snows, hails or rains hard, the keepers of the lights do not care to expose themselves . . ." It was after making these observations that Hutchinson went on to design the illuminating apparatus for his towers at Leasowe and Bidston.

Whatever the reasons for Trinity House's disinterest, Joseph Nelson was sent to build a new circular tower to replace the burned-out wreckage of Lutwige's lighthouse at St Bees. It cost £2,322 and was a fine, parallel-sided, rendered stone tower, painted white and illuminated by the argand burners and reflectors standard at the time. These were changed to a flashing character in the mid-nineteenth century and the present optic dates from 1951, an electric-powered lamp of 1500 watts amplified by a catadioptric lens which gives a group of two white flashes every twenty seconds. The intensity of the light is 146,000 candelas and it is visible twenty-one miles away on a clear, dark night. St Bees Head is of particular interest to ornithologists as upon its mellow sandstone cliffs is the only English breeding colony of black guillemots.

To the west of St Bees, the distant blue summit of Snaefell on the Isle of Man can be seen on a clear day. To the north, beyond the sandbanks and shifting channels of the Solway Firth whose name is already taking on the dialect of Scotland, lie the green hills of Kirkudbright. Rising behind St Bees Head, Skiddaw looms over a flat and rather ugly coastal plain, level above diminishing cliffs which gradually waste away between Whitehaven and Silloth. Here are the pitheads of the under-sea coalfield of Cumbria, a dark coast, reminiscent of its counterpart in Northumbria. The little ports that grew up to serve the industrial revolution now struggle to survive. Whitehaven and Workington on the lovely River Derwent remain viable, as does Silloth; but Maryport is largely silted, choked by the grim, coal-bearing spoil brought north-east by the beach-drift.

It was at Whitehaven that the American rebel naval captain John Paul Jones, whom we met off Flamborough Head, first made his name known to the British. He was born the son of a gardener who worked on the estates of the Earl of Selkirk, just across the Firth in Kirkudbrightshire. He went to sea as a boy and became an accomplished seaman, successfully navigating home a ship whose master and mate had both died. He rose to command his own merchant ship but a mutiny among the crew broke out, during which he had the "misfortune" to kill its ringleader. Rather than face trial, he went to the American colonies where his brother lived. As a seaman, he was able to fit out a ship of war and in the fall of 1775 he was the first American naval officer to raise the Grand Union, the Continental flag of Congress and later the first to have it saluted by a foreign power (ironically the French Royal Navy in Quiberon Bay, who were shortly to rue their encouragement of republicanism). Jones embarked on a series of cruises against British and loyalist trading vessels in which he was very successful. It was not long before he decided to carry the war further. In the early hours of 23 April 1778 (the newspapers were not slow to point out the shame of invasion upon St George's Day) he landed at Whitehaven and spiked the ancient cannon in the port's defensive batteries but his attempt to burn the shipping in the harbour was foiled. Nevertheless, he had struck a blow to British prestige. Next, he crossed the Solway and landed on the Earl of Selkirk's estate, hoping to take his lordship prisoner as a ransomable hostage. The Earl was absent and the Countess behaved with admirable coolness as Jones and his ruffianly crew of some thirty men dined at her table and insisted on carrying off her plate. (To his credit, Jones returned the plate afterwards at his own expense.) The next day he captured a small British man-of-war off Carrickfergus and returned to Brest a hero. It was as a result of this cruise that Benjamin Franklin, then American Ambassador to France, obtained for him the *Bonhomme Richard* in which he defeated Captain Pearson off Flamborough Head in 1779.

After the formation of the independent United States Jones acted on several diplomatic missions for Congress and whilst on one of these in Denmark, accepted an offer of employment as a rear-admiral in the Russian navy of Catherine the Great. A victim of court intrigue, he was disgraced even though he had won several victories over the Turks. He went to Paris a broken man, ignored by Congress, and died in poverty in July 1792. It was a century before his remains were taken to Annapolis where they became a naval shrine in the land of his adoption.

Another seaman whose reputation has, like Jones's, been greatly romanticized came from Maryport. Fletcher Christian has achieved the status of a hero largely because of the controversial character of the captain against whom he led a mutiny in 1779. Much has been written about the mutiny on board His Majesty's Armed Transport *Bounty*, some of it by Sir John Barrow. Yet there were far more horrifying, bloody and justified mutinies in the Royal Navy than that aboard a small and insignificant ship bound on a rather dubious mission to obtain cheap food for West Indian slaves. "Captain" Bligh was only a lieutenant at the time, but more is said of his character in the 4,000 miles voyage he made in an open boat following the mutiny, than in the real hard evidence against him as a sadistic tyrant. Few of those for whom the mutiny on the *Bounty* has been an irresistible theme have taken proper account of the fact that the probable reason for the sudden, spontaneous mutiny was not so much Bligh's uncompromising discipline, but the effect of the deliciously loose-moralled women of the South Pacific! Bligh was a pig-headed, irritant reminder of a harsh world when they had just left paradise. To such a keg of powder only a spark was needed, and the thwarted sexual drive of a crew of repressed seamen led by a young man who all agree was hopelessly in love, seems a much more plausible reason for revolt than the sadism of a man who both before and afterwards proved himself a seaman of uncommon ability.

A third local seaman was Joseph Huddart, born at Allonby near Maryport in 1741. Although his name is virtually unknown, countless hundreds of seamen had cause to be grateful to him for his work in improving anchor moorings. Little is known of his early life but he served in the East India ships of the Honourable East India Company in which he rose to command. He carried out some hydrographic surveying in the east and was clearly of a semi-scientific turn of mind. Huddart once witnessed the loss of a ship on a lee-shore and this affected him considerably, to such an extent that he determined to devise a safer form of anchor cable. He is credited with the invention of "cable-laid rope", that is special rope made of twisting, or laying-up, three ropes together, which achieved greater strength than a single large rope of a similar diameter. This increased the safety factor when a ship was anchored on a rough and abrasive bottom. He later set up as a rope-maker in London and extended his business to the manufacture of chains which began to replace rope for anchor cables in the early 1800s. It is perhaps not surprising to learn that Huddart was an Elder Brother of Trinity House and supplied chain cable for the moorings of lightvessels!

St Bees is the last English lighthouse on the west coast. Beyond Maryport and Silloth the coast seems to diminish, fading into the flat marshes of the border, watered by the estuaries of the Wampool, the Eden, the Waver and the Lyne. The sea and land merge in the salt-marsh beloved by feeding waders, where the piercing cry of the oystercatcher, borne on a chill wind, can seem like the most haunting sound imaginable. Here the sea invades the sinking land and the Solway, like the Severn, boasts its bore. "The tide advances with such rapidity upon the fatal sands that well-mounted horsemen lay aside hopes of safety if they see its white surge advancing while they are yet at a distance from the shore." So wrote Sir Walter Scott in *Redgauntlet*, but in the main the sea's victory is quieter here than where it strikes granite and limestone headlands.

The inevitable process of attrition continues quite regardless of man, yet everywhere there is evidence of his endeavours. From time to time, his works have had an effect upon the process itself, like the reclamation of north Norfolk by the Cokes that had such a disastrous consequence upon the little ports of Wells and Cley, or the sea wall at Lowestoft that resulted in the destruction of Pakefield. At the end of the nineteenth century 650,000 tons of shingle were removed from the foreshore behind Start Point, to be used in the construction of Devonport Dockyard. On 26 January 1917 an easterly gale and high tide combined to destroy the little village of Hallsands, left unprotected by its shingle barrier. Defences, whether against the sea or against enemies, form a prominent part of the human contribution to the appearance of the coast. Like the stumps of old teeth, the fortifications of successive generations remind us of the continuous presence of enmity.

Today it is on the margins of the sea that we isolate the nuclear power-stations of which we have such a desperate need, yet regard with mingled fear and suspicion. As architecture they are uniformly ugly, monuments to utilitarianism; but they cannot fail to impress. Both castles and nuclear power-stations are highly visible, many denoted on charts by the adjective "conspicuous" much beloved by hydrographers. Less obvious are the comings and goings of those who have made our history and therefore us. Viewed from the sea, this legacy of rebellions, flights, executions, marriages, murders and all the haughty business of the great and influential is not irrelevant. But neither are the contributions to the safety of seamen made by successive generations of lighthouse keepers.

These men have emerged as a special breed, highly individual and united only by their reliability. They are often diversely talented; authors, ornithologists, radio experts, artists, graduates, photographers, poets. Most are married with wives and families ashore where they hope eventually to end their service on one of the attractive land-stations that may survive into the next century. And their wives should not be forgotten. In an age which seeks to overturn the old adage that "men must work and women weep", reform comes late to jobs that involve separation and distance, usually manifesting itself in the unwelcome form of automation and redundancy. It is probable that the lighthouse will soon disappear as a purely visual aid to navigation. Electronic systems of position fixing are already in existence which threaten this. Perhaps the most up to date lighthouse in service today will be as anachronistic a hundred years hence as the coal chauffer seemed to Hutchinson and Stevenson.

But for sheer grandeur and nobility, of all the works of men upon the sea coast, almost rivalling nature itself in their claim upon our attention, the lighthouses remain unique. Symbolic of reliability, their construction is a tale of persistance and vision, courage and physical endurance. They are bold and largely successful attempts to mitigate the hazards of putting to sea and disarming the dangers of the coast. They are not immutable, of course; like Shelley's statue of Ozymandias, time will destroy them; the sea will undermine their foundations and consume them in the end. For ultimately the sea's challenge to mankind's ingenuity is eternal.

ACKNOWLEDGEMENTS
AND BIBLIOGRAPHICAL NOTE

We wish to express our gratitude to H.R.H. The Prince Philip, Duke of Edinburgh and Master of Trinity House, for his kindness in providing a foreword for this book.

We also wish to thank Sir Miles Wingate, KCVO, and the Board of Trinity House for their co-operation in making this joint venture possible.

It is a formidable task to thank individually the many members of the Trinity House Service who have helped either one or both of us in the production of this book. Their contributions, whether large or small, have been much appreciated by us but are too numerous to itemise in detail. We trust that we are forgiven this omission. However, acknowledgement must be made of the assistance and support we received from Paul Ridgway, Public Relations Officer of Trinity House, who far exceeded the call of duty in helping our project.

For those readers interested in following further the history and development of lighthouses, the following books were among the many sources used in the preparation of the text:

The World's Lighthouses before 1820, D. Alan Stevenson (OUP, 1959).

The Red Rocks of Eddystone, F. Majdalany (Longman's, Green, 1959).

The Lights of East Anglia, Neville Long (Terence Dalton, 1983).

English Lighthouse Tours of Robert Stevenson, D. Alan Stevenson (Thomas Nelson, 1946).

Keepers of the Sea, Richard Woodman (Terence Dalton, 1983).

Trinity House, Commander Hilary Mead (Samson Low).

The most useful source book for the coast itself was J. A. Steer's *The English Coast and the Coast of Wales* (Fontana, 1966). Inspired by the original "Operation Neptune" it seems most appropriate to mention this laudable project for the preservation of Britain's coastline in the year of its revival.

David Smith
Richard Woodman

INDEX